HOW DIVORCE BECAME MY DELIVERANCE

ELONA WASHINGTON | AMANDA GARCIA | C. MICHELLE ATKINS
DANNIELLE BROWN | LISA MCGOVERN | LORI OBAYOMI NISHA |
STEPHANIE THOMAS | TRACEE UPTON

Philadelphia, PA

Copyright © 2017 Elona Washington
All rights reserved. No part of this book may be reproduced in any form or by any electronic or mechanical means, including information storage and retrieval systems, with or without permission from the publisher or author, except in the case of a reviewer, who may quote brief passages embodied in critical articles or in a review.

Some names and identifying details have been altered to protect individual privacy.

Image designed by Alan Cotton

Book design and production by
Memoir Maven Publishing

ISBN-13: 978-0692957868

ISBN-10: 0692957863

Table of Contents

Foreword Andrea M. Stuckey	VI
Introduction Dannielle Brown	10
Chapter 7 C. Michelle Atkins	13
1.....Longing For Love Lisa McGovern	15
2.....My Journey To Joy Dannielle Brown	31
3.....He Did Us A Favor Amanda Garcia	45
4.....The Un-Relationship C. Michelle Atkins	60
5.....Smoke And Mirrors And Marriage Lori Obayomi	75
6.....I Ain't Sayin She A Gold Digger... Nisha	96
7.....Lessons From The Other Side Stephanie Thomas	108
8.....Things Aren't Always What They Seem Tracee Upton	128
9.....It Had To Happen Elona Washington	143
Afterword Elona Washington	158
Freedom C. Michelle Atkins	162
Get Support	163
About The Authors	164

Foreword

"Be strong and of good courage, do not fear nor be afraid of them; for the Lord our God, He is the One who goes with you. He will not leave you nor forsake you." Deuteronomy 31:6

Divorce is a major life altering event. Yet, despite the stigma and its harrowing effects, approximately 50% of marriages end in divorce. And no amount of preparation can make such a transition any less painful. Having been divorced twice in two very different seasons of my life, I resonate with many of the stories provided in this book.

How Divorce Became My Deliverance is an excellent compilation of a range of experiences that led these women to the state of divorce. Despite the abuse, abandonment, and lack of love, their decision to divorce was not an easy one, and they share a plethora of information as to the events which led them to such a life altering resolve.

In my experience of two marriages and two divorces, I too suffered the trauma of abandonment, physical, emotional and verbal abuse, just as many of the contributors to this book. Oftentimes, abusive marriages and even the subsequent divorce leave the residue of rejection, loss, low self- esteem and low self-worth. Through my personal relationship with God, years of counseling and coaching, I overcame many of those residual effects. And it is because of my experience that my purpose is to connect with women through personal coaching and events to help them regain their power, find peace, rebuild their lives, and walk into the greatness that God has for them.

Individual personal development is a major key to overcoming the pain and tragedy of divorce. It is evident that the authors did the work; their transparency and resilience is a testament to it. How Divorce Became My Deliverance is a powerful anthology of women sharing heartfelt experiences, and tragedies in addition to their victories and life epiphanies. Written by women of various backgrounds and life experiences, it's easy for any divorcée to identify with their pain and the lessons learned. I encourage every woman, divorced or not, to pick up this book. You won't regret it.

*****

"Know that divorce is not the end all be all. You can live again, love again, and embrace all that this life has to offer."

Andrea M. Stuckey

*****

Andrea M. Stuckey is the Founder of Live Life Luvd Coaching LLC, a Speaker and Author of *Suddenly Single: A Woman's Spiritual & Practical Guide to the First Five Years Following Separation and Divorce.*

Introduction

Deliverance is defined as the act of being rescued or set free. This book is aptly titled although, at one time, we considered our marriage to be deliverance from a life of loneliness. What followed, though, was a union with an unequally yoked spouse and because of it, some of us found the strength to walk away while others ultimately learned to heal from the abandonment. The tables are now reversed and we have found ourselves delivered from marriage and once again, set free.

Throughout our marriages and even after, our knees knew the pain from constant prayer and mourning and for some, our make up served to cover up not only blemishes but bruises too. Each story differs greatly from the other, but as you read them all, you will notice that instead of the dream of a lifelong marriage, what arose instead was an awakening, an incredible sense of strength, an overflow of joy...survival at its finest. From it, each author discovered the true definition of love and grew from the painful lessons our loveless and/or abusive marriages taught.

These nine authors come from a myriad of backgrounds. They each traveled different paths, but ended up in the same place, answering the same question, "How do I survive, collect my pieces of the puzzle, and put the inner me back together again?" From their respective answers, they rose from the ashes of infidelity, neglect, physical, emotional and financial abuse. Today, a fire burns from the lessons they learned and they each relish in their new found spirit of peace, joy, and resiliency.

Remember, this book was written with you in mind. Its purpose is to incite in you a spirit of conqueror...not defeat, survival...not despair, over comer...not failure. If you empathize with the stories compiled in this anthology and your marriage has dissolved or is in the process of ending, despite how you feel, please know, you will not only survive, you will thrive. Consider yourself fortunate, even if you're functioning in a barren place. It may not feel like it right now; at one time it surely didn't for us, but divorce can be a welcoming release, a second chance, an opportunity to begin again. So journey into these authors' hearts and feel the pulse of their change, their healing, self love, and the granddaddy of them all...*wholeness*. Ironically, divorce became our *unexpected* deliverance.

Dannielle Brown
Masters Counseling Psychology 2017 Candidate

Chapter 7

No money for a lawyer, but I filed bankruptcy

Cashed in on a relationship that was killing me inside...

pain so deep I could no longer hide

Chapter 7 was the only way out

Stuck in debt...too much invested but not enough return

Bills so high stacked well above my head

Trying hard every month just to survive

No extra coming in but more going out

Lives and well being were at stake

Chapter 7 was my only means to an end

It put an end to the worry of How?

And reassured me that I Can

Now I have a fresh start...

A brand new beginning

A chance to rebuild my credit and credibility

I have a chance to build a New Life

Thank you Chapter 7...thank you

C. Michelle Atkins

Chapter 7 is from the book entitled, *Tales from My Life, not the Crypt*, by C. Michelle Atkins, copyright 2014.

Longing For Love

After only a few minutes, my name was called and once again, I made my way to the registration desk. This time, a nurse led me through security doors and into a private area. She stopped, asked me to remove all of my clothes, laid paper pajamas on a steel chair, and left the room. I obeyed. And I cried. When the nurse returned, she collected my belongings and took me down an even longer hallway. She stopped at one of the doors and held her arm out suggesting that this would be my room and I should enter. Usually, that motion is inviting and you anticipate stepping into a plush hotel room or checking out the amazing view from a cruise ship cabin. Not this time. I had voluntarily checked myself into Prince George's County (Maryland) Hospital's Psychiatric Center and she had escorted me to my room: an austere space with colorless walls and no windows, electrical outlets or decorations.

I was having a mental breakdown and needed to get away. But if you spoke to my friends and family, they would claim that it's been going on for years. And in a sense, they would be correct. All my life, I've had this longing to be loved. I was raised by a drug-addicted mother, my siblings and I aren't close, and in the beginning of my life, my dad wasn't around at all. As an adult, I was reunited with him for only a few years. He passed away. So I grew up around a mother and siblings who only cared about what I could do for them. From the moment I got a job at the age of 14, all they did was beg for money. They were all irresponsible, so if they managed to get a job, they spent their money frivolously. And when they found themselves in a bind, they expected me to solve it. And when I did, I wouldn't hear from them again until their next catastrophe. Neither ever offered to hang out or get our children together; after a few minutes of small talk, they'd get right to their sob story. Although I've felt used for years, as the eldest, I never refused them.

They are my family despite the fact that all eight of us had different fathers and, to this day, they have yet to return the favor.

My family though, was not the reason I checked myself into a psych ward; I was there because of my husband. Steven and I had been friends for twenty years; we had dated on and off for the first five years before settling into a platonic friendship. Throughout those years, he married, had children and divorced. Twice. I was his shoulder to cry on and his ear to listen to it all. So yes, I knew he had cheated on wife #1 and when he married wife #2, he cheated again. While still married to wife #2, he fathered his last child with the latest in a series of booty calls. Although wife #2 forgave him and desired to make the marriage work, he divorced her anyway. He always accused his exes of being crazy but I dismissed him because most men call women that.

A few months after his second divorce, Steven and I were chatting on the phone and speculating as to why we're both still single when the conversation took a different turn. I was spending all of my free time and finances taking care of my mother due to her poor health. I had recently moved in with her so I could provide additional care and she was stressing me out. That's when he offered to take care of me in return. Given he was already there for me emotionally and financially, I knew what he was insinuating. Steven was flirting with me. I gave in just a bit; I wasn't not easy. I told him that I was celibate and wouldn't have sex again until I was a wife. So we discussed the possibility of marriage and believed that the two of us could make it work. A few months later, we donned Washington Redskins jerseys and headed to the Virginia County Courthouse to be married. Feeling ecstatic, we left the courthouse and drove to Georgetown to celebrate our union with designer desserts from Georgetown Cupcakes. Neither our courtship nor marriage was traditional but our friendship was solid and he had proven his loyalty and love for me time and time again.

Steven was the first person I confided in when I was diagnosed HIV+. He kept my secret and when I would get sick, he dropped everything to take care of me. He understood what it meant to be married to me and was willing to be there when I needed him. I believed I had married my savior and protector, a man who truly loved me. Isn't that what love really is?

    What I didn't realize was when I married Steven, I also married into ruinous family drama. His two ex-wives and baby mother were more than crazy. They were conniving, vengeful and nefarious. They were infuriated when they learned we wed because I'd been a cause of dissension throughout their respective relationships. Each had accused us of having an affair because Steven would drop everything when I needed him. Their accusations never bothered me because, aside from a brief fling we had when he was married to wife #1, it simply wasn't true. And, even though I was well aware of his past and their current state of loathing for me, I trusted him when he was around the mothers of his children and gave him space when he wanted to spend time with his kids. He was an excellent father to his six children and he really wanted to be there for them. To him, fatherhood wasn't only about providing financially; it also meant playing an active role in their lives. Steven made every attempt to attend practices, games, school performances, etc. and if they fell ill, he worked to be by their side. His wives were aware of his devotion and exploited it at every turn. The perpetual games they played as well as Steven's own behavior were not only driving a wedge between us, it was driving me crazy.

Ex-wife #1 lived out of state and called the house daily to harass me. She screeched repeatedly into the phone that Steven never loved me and he only married me for my money. She added that he wasn't going to be faithful because he still loved her and our marriage would never work because I couldn't have any more children. Her accusations never bothered me because she was wrong on all fronts, especially with regard to my infertility. Steven desperately wanted us to have a child, but I refused. I didn't want to risk contracting him/her with HIV. So when she called, I gave it to her right back. I wasn't timid or afraid of her. But once I realized she'd never stop harassing me, I blocked her numbers so she could only contact Steven via his cell. Then she got their children to call and cuss me out instead. She knew I wouldn't dare block their numbers so everyday when the phone rang, it immediately sent me into fight or flight mode. Your home should be a peaceful retreat after a stressful day, not a daily battleground. But Steven refused to listen to how the harassment was making me feel.

    We were only married three months when ex-wife #2 dropped off her three children to live with us. Two of the kids weren't even his! But Steven didn't care; he welcomed his former stepchildren into our home so I did too. While we provided for them, she made every attempt to run my home. When I discovered their daughter had been skipping school and spending time with a boy, I punished her by taking away her phone. Ex-wife #2 showed up unannounced at my door and scorched me for disciplining her daughter. She screamed I had no right to do so and proceeded to cuss me out in my home in front of the children and Steven. As she slammed my door on her way out, I instinctively ran after her. By the look on my face, Steven knew I wanted to whoop that ass. But he restrained me and asked, "you aren't being godly...is that what Jesus would do?" He didn't even bother to calm me down! I stormed off and spent the rest of the evening in the bedroom. I was in tears. He came into the room later and claimed he chastised her about her behavior, but I never received an apology and her behavior certainly didn't change. He walked out without acknowledging my feelings of anger and frustration regarding the matter. He simply expected me to take it. Her kids lasted three months with us -- while she received court-ordered child support the entire time.

The "booty call," as I like to refer to her, wasn't permitted to call our home unless her daughter was visiting. Her communication with Steven had to be via text or email only. This was all court ordered! When their daughter visited, booty call ordered her to not to eat my cooking, talk or even look at me. She wasn't allowed to come near me, get in my car and talk to her father if I was within earshot. Her pettiness wasn't acknowledged though; I dismissed all that foolishness and helped their daughter with her homework, washed her clothes, bathed, fed her and did her hair. Once, booty call drove her own daughter to tears when she discovered we were snuggled up on the couch watching TV. After yelling and cursing the little girl out, she ordered her to go to her room, close the door, and stay away from me. She proceeded to call Steven and cuss him out over it and threatened to call the police and report that I was abusing their baby.

 Everything I described was happening daily, simultaneously, and through it all, Steven had ceased being my lover, partner and friend. I became his doormat. If his exes or kids needed something, he dropped everything in our home and headed to comfort and meet their needs. Not once did he complain or refuse their requests. And it left me feeling lonely and hurt. One evening, for example, Steven walked into the bedroom and looked me dead in my face. It was apparent I was crying. Tears and mucus were running down my face and nose and I was still weeping. It was the anniversary of my father's passing; not once did he ask what's wrong or if I needed anything. Years ago, when he was my friend, he would have sat there and comforted me even if I claimed nothing was wrong. Steven had turned a new, careless leaf and it left me dumbfounded. I didn't know who he was anymore and I resented him for all the pain and drama he, his ex-wives, baby mama and children were causing.

When we first wed, I didn't work for 18 months but when I returned to the workforce, I used my earnings to get him out of debt, ignoring my own debt. He hadn't filed taxes in years and when the repayment letters came in, he refused to pay them, explaining he needed to give his children money first. So I took care of it. The children to which he was referring were grown and in college. He insisted on playing the role of "big daddy" and worked tirelessly to pay their tuition so they wouldn't have to rely on student loans. With the amount of debt we were both facing, we did not have the income to take on such a responsibility. One evening, as I was sitting at the kitchen table paying his bills, I asked him why he stopped being there for me. I was surprised he even responded but he explained that he felt guilty for not being a full-time dad. I replied that it was a weak excuse for why he suddenly stopped being my friend. Then I asked, "why did you stop being my friend? His response: silence.

    Steven never answered my question so I could only surmise that he subconsciously created the same environment in which he was raised. His mother became addicted to drugs after the death of his father and according to family members, never was the same. According to them, she appeared unemotional and detached. Steven never knew his biological father; he was an infant when his father passed. His stepfather had been in his life since he was six months old and Steven always saw him as the financial provider. He couldn't recall his dad ever showing love or affection toward his mother. She was a full-time homemaker so when his dad would arrive home, there was always a hot, fancy meal waiting for him. Steven and his siblings ate meals like hot dogs and beans instead. They were pretty much ignored and I think it hurt him that his parents cared so little for them, he strived to be a better father. But when it came to marriage, he didn't bother to do anything differently. He only wanted to provide financially and expected me to remain stoic as I took care of the house, the kids and his emotional and physical needs.

Eventually, I did what every woman does when she wants to make their marriage work: I sought counseling. I didn't believe he'd agree, but I received no push back from him at all. For more than a year, our counselor worked to improve our communication skills and provided objective input when it came to his exes and children. It seemed as if we were making progress. When we first married in 2011, I had told Steven I wanted our bedroom painted purple, my favorite color. Steven never got around to doing it although he worked to meet the littlest needs of his kids and exes. The counselor managed to explain to him that the simple task of painting the room would make me happy. Having money in the bank wasn't enough. It looked as if a light bulb went off in his head. But my joy was soon overshadowed with despair. The counselor then asked him to list the reasons why he loved me. He had no answer. And even more heart-wrenching was that he didn't provide an answer until a year later. He confessed that I was the only woman who worked for and put in an effort towards the marriage. So, just like my mom and siblings, he didn't truly love me. He loved what I did for him, how I made him feel. I satisfied Steven's love language but he had no interest in learning and supplying mine. And further proof was given when he visited me in the psych ward. He looked uncomfortable as he sat in the visitor's station. Smiling sheepishly, I approached him and sat down to talk, hoping for comforting and encouraging words from him. Instead, his voice was irritated, impatient. Then he flat out stated that I didn't belong "in there" and that he would have never considered me a weak woman. I'd been the rock of the family for years and he didn't know what he needed to do to fix things. After explaining that there would need to be outpatient counseling to help us through it, he shook his head as if he understood. Visitation over, he walked out without hugging me or holding my hand. I never saw him again.

With nowhere else to go, I moved in with my mother and a couple of siblings who never moved out. I got a job and again, was the only responsible person in the house. Each time I refused to give my mother money, or if I simply didn't have it, she threatened to kick me out. Desperate for a change of pace, scenery, and peace, I relocated to Dallas to be near my daughter and son-in-law. Tiffany was the product of my first marriage, and he never loved me either. We were young and dating casually when I got pregnant. His parents were religious and regular church members. They insisted we marry even though they knew we weren't in love and that their son slept around with other women. They didn't care. They just wanted to look good for the congregation. We divorced before our second wedding anniversary.

My entire life, I worked overtime to make others happy and expected the same in return. Life should have taught me otherwise a long time ago but finally, I got it. This time around, I'm putting me first. That's not selfish. It's self love. I can't expect someone to love and treat me well if I continue to accept less. Never again will I allow another family member, friend or loved one to use or treat me badly.

My Journey To Joy

I thought I would be married for a lifetime to the love of my life. For 19 years and 4 months, I had known one man, Mr. Q. Mr. Q was the gatekeeper of my dreams, aspirations, and hope enveloped in pride as a wife, mother, and friend. Within the gates of our marriage, I rendered myself freely, thinking it was necessary for the security of the roles. I thought I hit the jackpot. No, he wasn't rich, but he had potential, stability, and a degree from the same university (Howard University) from which I also graduated. I yielded to him physically and spiritually being caught up in the rapture of promises made, vows spoken, and heartache. I understood fully the vows "for better or for worse and until death do us apart" which I openly confessed on Christmas Eve. I promise you, this woman was all in and loyal to the core. I was committed to our marriage. Regrettably, death came in the form of divorce. Yes I still had breath, but I had to learn to breathe again. I don't mean to sound like a line in one of my favorite movies "Diary of a Mad Black Woman", but Mr. Q was my everything.

I was working at the Howard University Career Services Center in the Summer of 1992 when I watched this confident man enter the office, drop off some paperwork, flirt, book me (ask for my number), and leave. I stared out of the office window and followed him with my eyes as he walked down the street out of my view. At the time, I was on the office phone with my best friend, Cornita. I prophesied to her; I had just met the man I would love to marry one day. Funny right? I had just spoken this marriage into existence. I was smitten by his charm and attracted to his personality. He possessed both academic and street smarts. I too was attractive, smart, and had my share of fans on campus. Mr. Q and I had very little contact from 1992 to 1995. During that time, I was involved in a relationship with a high school ex, and had a son. After dropping out of college for a few years, I managed to refocus my life and return to Howard in the fall of 1993. I also started dating Mr. Q in 1995 and fell in love.

When I fell in love, I simultaneously divorced myself. I became everything I thought I should be to him. We had unbelievable chemistry and because of those strong feelings; I wanted him to accept my son as his own. Mr. Q accepted him and I birthed him a son, and on Christmas Eve 1997, I became his wife. I loved being a wife and was very happy to be Mrs. Brown. I knew I was called to be a wife and a mom to our two strong-minded boys. Just when things seemed absolutely perfect, life happened...

I could share all the things that went wrong that lead to our demise. The pendulum could have shifted to either side. We ran the whole gamut in our relationship, from being a successful couple to living in despair. There were addictions, mental health, infidelity, lying, deception, failures, disappointments, and physical abuse. Yep, there are two sides to every story and I assure you Mr. Q would disagree with parts of my truth. It's not my job to refute what Mr. Q would say in this matter. I am speaking my truth. If I was a spider who spun the web to house herself in the corner of the ceiling, protected from reach, but in full view of the dose of poison our marriage took in daily, the spider would paint this picture-a successful couple, attractive family, and a lifestyle few would not experience in their early to mid-twenties. We did a lot and amassed a lot before reaching the age of 30. We had homes, apartment buildings, substantial bonus checks, and we were well on our way to executing the formula to generational wealth. Our net worth was something that made us both proud.

    Mr. Q had graduated a few years before me so he

had already started his career. In the beginning of our marriage, Mr. Q was Mr. Perfect. He spoiled me. He made sure I graduated from college and moved me into his home located down the street from Howard University. The move closer to campus made it easier for me to finish my degree. From the outside, our marriage had all the ingredients to be a success. However, we were flawed. I wore the glasses that only allowed me to see roses and beauty while the spider in the corner saw the truth. For so long, my insides were screaming. Silence gripped by fear suppressed the emotions from surfacing and exposing me to the harsh reality that I was dying right along with my marriage. To escape, to hang on to a thin thread of life, I turned to journaling. Journaling allowed me to release my emotions and to talk to God. I let the pen scream, cry, and be raw with every emotion you can imagine from a deeply rooted painful place. I wanted my marriage to work at all costs. I was very much in love with Mr. Q. I did everything I could to win his love and approval. I even took the

"Excellent Wife" class at church in which I was honored by the class with a certificate for my outstanding contribution. I attended the Wives Support Group, was mentored by other married women of faith, and read multitudes of books related to marriage. My two favorite books I read daily were by Stormie Omartian, Praying Through the Deeper Issues of Marriage and The Power of a Praying Wife. Yep, I also did the Fire Proof challenge and loved the movie War Room. I was a nurturer in my marriage. I thought I could win by loving hard, fasting, praying, and being loyal. However, my efforts were never good enough. I was never good enough. His thirst went unquenched because I wasn't the drink he desired.

In my assessment, we married young and we both lacked marital maturity-but lacking maturity seems to be the norm. Two people who marry young ought to grow in maturity together right? In our case, we lacked the marital tools and it caused us to grow in unhealthy directions. The unhealthiness was soo thick, it caused me to have a mental and emotional breakdown. I had to seek help. I kept soo much inside and I did not know how to release the pain. I self-sabotaged. I didn't want to die, but I did want to hurt myself. It was crazy; I thought I was crazy. The verbal and physical abuse was bad, but I cannot blame it all on Mr. Q. I was an active participant in the unhealthiness. Why did I fight for an unhealthy situation? Because I wanted my marriage to work. I loved him more than I loved myself. My rock bottom hit when I had to look into the eyes of my 3-year-old as he watched his mommy being taken to the hospital due to self-harm and emotional stress. This is where Mr. Q can go into more detail. I am sure what he would say will contain some elements of truth.

    Getting therapy as a result of my marriage was my saving grace-although I was the only participant. I felt the prayers of the few who knew our secrets willing me back to life. I had checked out and was in a very dark place. I thought about my children, and yes, even my husband. I had a lot of issues from my childhood I needed to resolve that had a huge influence on my behavior throughout the marriage. Through counseling, I began the journey of self-acceptance and self-love. I got stronger, better, and healthy. The most important thing: I realized I wasn't crazy. I had to learn to communicate and not be fearful. I walked on eggshells throughout my marriage and never felt valued. I used to ask Mr. Q often why he didn't value me. In time, I understood that he suffered from insecurities as a man. His failures and my lack of self-love became our family's punishment. I still fought for the marriage, but this time I fought for us to get the help we needed to be a healthy couple together. Mr. Q had mentally and physically checked out and checked in with others who weren't his wife. I was losing the battle.

Like doctors who are trying to resuscitate the dying;

someone had to call the time.....Feb 2, 2012. My marriage died, but unknowing to me, I was being born again into a life I had never known...joy.

For five years, I retreated from the world and focused on raising my two young men with little help and support from Mr. Q. It was the darkest and the scariest of times. The question I constantly asked myself, "how do I pick up the pieces and survive?" I spent days and nights crying bitter tears. I had become accustomed to the salted taste of tears as I wept. There were numerous days when I was unable to get out of the bed. I did not know the sunrise from sunset. My boys escaped to their room, video games, cell phones, sports, and grandma's house-their solace and welcomed distraction. Very much exposed, my sons saw my pain, comforted me, and subsequently became the men of the home. The boys spoke life into me until I was strong enough to spoon feed my self-esteem. I had to learn to be healthy again, not to function as a robot, but as a mother, a woman. One thing for sure, I never stopped journaling.

My husband left us on February 2, 2012, and I received my divorce papers on March 11, 2015. I received my divorce papers on my 44th birthday. Cruel and insensitive, right? But he did what I could not do. I viewed marriage as a sacred institution and would have been committed to "death do us a part" regardless how I was treated. I was stuck on honoring my vows to the very end. Shamefully I admit, I didn't have self-love to know better or believe I deserved better. I spent the last five years being faithful, honoring God, rebuilding, discovering, enjoying, and loving myself. My prayers were focused prayers. I asked God to show me thyself and to give me a new love and a new hope-independent of a man. In my journals, it chronicled how God became my everything-my husband, daddy, friend, confidant, lover, teacher, provider, father to my children, heart fixer, and my absolute joy. Day by day, my joy was increasing and bursting at the seams.

From March 2015 to our final court date, April 12, 2017, Mr. Q and I had been fighting over our DC properties and finances. But guess what? Even in the worst of those times, I still had joy. God restored me and gave me joy. I experienced loss, sadness, and unfortunate circumstances, but yet I still had joy. When people betray you, life feels unfair, times get difficult, people walk out of your life, you feel lonely, and you feel sad, but you still got that inner ticking inside that supersedes the feelings of despair; you have joy!

Dear Mr. Q,

I have much gratitude towards you for pulling the plug to an unhealthy relationship and knowing that I was too loyal to do so. I sincerely thank you. You are a good person and I know you love your boys. I pray you have taken the time to work on yourself and find your truth which is nestled in inner peace. Our marriage was not soo much different than a lot of marriages today. There are many couples who are weathering the same storms and have a hidden compartment that holds their secrets too. I spend many days praying for marriages. I hope you can respect my transparency. I want my testimony to be a blessing to others in hope of saving someone from allowing the violence of divorce hinder their ability to have a fulfilled-joyful life. There is always your side of the story too and I respect that. I am free and I get to begin again. I have a new lease on life and I promise not to take it for granted. I hope your days are filled with joy and happiness. I wish you the best in life.

Ms. Dannie B

Lastly, most never have an opportunity to be their most authentic self. I know people who are older than I who are still trying to find themselves. I also know people who are stuck in bitterness, grief, and mishaps of life, and may very well die never experiencing joy. There are others that lost their joy and have not been able to get it back. My take home message from my experience with divorce: man is not responsible for my joy or can he extinguish it. My joy is an internal flame that speaks volumes to being whole and complete. It's a crazy type of love that allows you to look in the mirror and even on your worst day, you are still able to see inner beauty. I know others see it too and are attracted to the healthiness in me that screams in its own voice "I am no longer life happenstance. I am joy." It's done. Do not resuscitate. Call the time of death. I am ready to begin again!

He Did Us A Favor

It was December 23, 2015. All of the kids were jumping on the bed and shaking me frantically. They couldn't find their dad. Groggy, I didn't understand their sense of urgency. No, their father wasn't lying next to me, but I figured he left the house to run errands or handle business. Todd was an entrepreneur so he never let holidays impede a deal. He would get up and go whenever the client was ready to move forward. After more than 15 years together, I had grown accustomed to it. Our kids were teens and preteens at the time; I was under the impression they had too.

Irritated, I got up and looked around the bedroom. There was no sign of him anywhere...absolutely no sign of him. His shoes weren't in the middle of the floor. His cologne, jewelry and loose change were no longer on the dresser. I flew out of the bedroom and checked the hallways, the bathroom, and living room for any sign of him. Nothing. In a nervous panic, I raced back to the master bedroom and checked his closet. Please, please, please. I flung open the doors. Nothing. He even took the hangers! I was absolutely stunned. He moved all of his shit while we were asleep. After shock and amazement wore off, fury set in. Not only did he take his things, he also took my and the kids' Christmas gifts! Things between us were combative, even from the beginning, but I never thought he'd pull something like this! This pained me, yes, but it just about devastated our children.

I said "just about" because the kids were sick of him. Since Todd's mom passed away, he'd become cold and demeaning, resorting to emotional and physical abuse for every little thing they did or didn't do. Once, he was so angry at the eldest child, he called her a bitch because she cited scripture to prove that he was wrong. Before anyone could process what happened next, Todd was dragging her down the stairs by her leg! When they reached the landing, he looked as if he was going to hit her, but the kids and I hurried over and stepped in. He punched the youngest child in the chest and called him a mistake because he left his toys in the middle of the floor. He smacked another daughter upside the head for leaving the front door open; the kids were unloading groceries. The kids weren't just walking on eggshells for fear of his yelling; they were accustomed to his verbal abuse. They had become bothered by the emotional abuse he inflicted and frightened about what he would do to them physically.

    I was never emotionally abused or raised under the threat of physical violence and it certainly wasn't something I wanted my kids to endure. My mother was a devoted, sweet woman and my father loved her deeply. They raised me and my three sisters in a Christian household and used very little physical punishment. At 19, we lost them both unexpectedly and our home was never the same. My sisters and I were adults, but their loss put us in a depressive state and instead of bringing us closer, we went to war over the littlest things. The constant arguing, mourning, crying and stress was unbearable and I desperately to move. All our lives, we lived in an affluent California neighborhood, so it wasn't my intention to move into some ghetto apartment and struggle. That was all I could afford at the time so I stayed. Our parents left very generous wills which enabled us to pay off the house and go to college but we all got jobs to split the household bills and saved what remained. There was no dissension when it came to managing money; we weren't going to be careless and lose our home. I am realizing now that my parents' loss and desire to live comfortably fueled my decision to be with Todd. It was this vulnerability that drew me to Todd...or drew Todd to me. He was fine, don't get me wrong. He was tall, slender and had the deepest blue eyes I'd ever looked into. Unlike most Californians, he wasn't tanned at all. I liked that. From the moment he approached my table and introduced himself, everything about him, about us, seemed right. It felt like fate.

I was out having dinner with my girlfriends the night I met Todd. My sisters and I had another fight over something incredibly small and I left to vent with my friends. When Todd came over, we invited him to sit with us and he and I hit it off immediately. My friends slyly gave their approval and after paying our tab, I gave Todd my number. To say our relationship moved quickly would be an understatement. After dating only a few months, I moved in with him. Then I got pregnant. This was our first child and as soon as we settled into a routine. I was pregnant again. After the second child, I was ready to be married but Todd continued to stall. I had never been in a relationship before so not only was he the father of my children, he was the only man I had been with sexually. I loved him and couldn't fathom being with another man. We had to get married. To make my point clear, one night while he was away on business, the kids and I moved out of the home. I took everything: clothes, furniture, drapes, dishes, cutlery, etc Everything. Todd later shared that when he opened the front door, he was dumbstruck. He left and booked a room at a hotel. He tried calling me for days but because I wouldn't answer, he began pleading his case with my sisters. After hearing his side, they eventually begged me to return his call and when I did, he confessed that he didn't want to go through the pain of losing his family again. Aside from his mother, we were all he had. Then he asked me to marry him. I returned home and a few months later, we held a small ceremony in the backyard. Fifteen years later, my husband pulled the same shit on me and our five children.

    When Christmas Day arrived, the kids had forgotten all about the abandonment and honestly, didn't care about the toys because there was peace in our home. After opening the last-minute gifts I purchased, we spent the morning at church and the afternoon with friends. I couldn't bring myself to mention what we were going through so I sat around the kitchen table with the other wives while the kids ran outside to enjoy the California winter weather. The men assumed that Todd was away on business and I said nothing to the contrary. When we went home, I headed to the kitchen to prepare a traditional holiday meal. The shock was wearing off and my soul wanted to crawl into bed and cry. One of my boys took a break from his bike, ran into the kitchen, and gave me a hug. Then he exclaimed, "I don't need a father. You can be my mom and my dad." Tears swelled so I didn't reply right away. I just hugged him tightly and finally said, "I love you and we'll be OK." When dinner was ready, my children and I sat around the table enjoying our meal, laughing, and joking around. No one mentioned Todd at all.

  Months before he walked out on us, the children had been hinting for me to leave but I never took them seriously. The house was indeed tense and we weren't happy at all, but I never believed they wanted us to separate. My children had known no other way of life. While Todd had always been stern and verbally abusive, he had reached a new low with the emotional and physical abuse. I figured it would stop once he came to terms with his mother's death but it was approaching a year since her loss and he was only getting worse. Todd and his mom were very close, and because I shared the same relationship with my mother, I empathized with his pain. Yet, I never condoned his behavior. I urged him to go to counseling but he refused. One day, while Todd was home behaving like a tyrant, one of my daughters texted me a GIF of a woman pushing money from the palm of her hand, "making it rain." I was confused, so I texted back, "What's this for?"

"You need to get your weight up and leave that man." Notice how she didn't say her dad?

My daughter's text message brought up another problem. How could I afford to pay the mortgage and bills on a 5,000 square foot home? I never finished college and was a stay-at-home mom until about five years ago. There was no way I could pay the bills on my administrative assistant salary. Shortly after the "making it rain" GIF,

Todd returned my calls and promised to send money every week. But it was sent sporadically, so I couldn't rely on it. His next solution was for me to use the credit cards and he'd pay off the balance. This was a huge help, especially with the kids needing so much. Fortunately, the kids understood the gravity of our situation and helped out the best they could. Without me ever asking, the teen girls picked up babysitting jobs and everyone stepped up around the house. There were plenty of evenings I'd walk into a spotless home with dinner waiting. I was blessed to have such amazing children.

  Spring arrived and I realized I was happy that he was gone. While his emotional abuse of the children was new to them, it wasn't new to me. During our courtship, he spoiled me and treated me like a queen, but once we married, he turned vicious. He called me ugly almost everyday and made fun of my dark skin. He joked that I needed to stay out of the sun or if the lights were off, he'd ask me to smile so he could see me. He constantly reminded me that no one would want someone so dark, fat and dumb, especially with five kids. He showed me pictures of his exes and bragged about how much prettier they were than I. It shook me to my core but instead of showing it, I learned to be just as cruel to him. But honestly, the damage had been done. My self-esteem was in the toilet. But with Todd out of the house, it slowly started to return. I noticed I was smiling and laughing more, wearing makeup and more flattering clothes. During a girls' night out, some of my friends even mentioned that I no longer walked with my head down.

    When summer vacation started, the kids began asking to see their father so we made arrangements for them to spend the summer with him and his new girlfriend. Todd had fallen in love and moved in with some woman months after leaving our home. His new love didn't influence his old ways though. Every time we spoke, he reminded me how stupid or weak or fat I was. When we'd hang up, he'd send text messages threatening me to sue me, throw me in jail and get full custody of the kids. He also warned that I'd get nothing from him and he'd make sure that I go bankrupt and end up on the street. While I ignored his rants and never responded to his texts, I kept record of them all. I even downloaded a voice record app on my phone which transferred our conversations to the cloud. His words no longer hurt and I intended to use them to my advantage. His threats about keeping the children didn't bother me either. Deep down, I knew he didn't want the responsibility. When the kids left, I picked up a part-time job and spent the little free time I had recharging. The kids were wonderful but they were a lot. For years, I hadn't spent any time focusing on me and I desperately needed some self care. I wasn't fat but I was out of shape so I joined a gym and made an appointment at a natural hair salon. I was finally going to go natural. I also called my pastor and relayed everything that had been going on. He recommended that I start seeing a counselor and I was actually looking forward to doing so.

The kids checked in regularly and reported that everything was fine. About a week later, however, I received the first troubling call from my eldest son. He was incoherent and crying uncontrollably. After calming him down, he explained that dad told him someone was going to break in and rape me. He wanted to come home. I talked to him for over an hour, reassuring him that nothing was going to happen to me. The daughter who sent the "make it rain" GIF called shortly after thoroughly disgusted. Todd had told her that he was having the best sex of his life and every time he reached orgasm, he felt like he was in heaven. Then, my eldest daughter told me she asked to go to church and he refused. He began yelling and accused me and my mother of being Christian whores and he wasn't going to have her turn out like me. There were more plenty more incidents, but when I learned that Todd told our youngest child that he would have beat my ass if I wasn't a Christian, I knew it was time for them to come home. The kids had lasted less than a month with their dad.

You would think Todd would have been finished, but he was just getting started. Soon after the kids returned, I walked out of the house to discover that the SUV was towed. The truck was in Todd's name, but he had agreed to let me keep it because of the children. Of course, I wasn't given notice; he wanted to piss me off and inconvenience me. I took off work that day and a friend drove me to a dealership. I bought my own damn truck. A week later, local cops were at my door warning me that I could be arrested tonight. Terrified, I listened as one cop explained that my husband was charging me with identity theft. He claimed we were legally separated and I had no legitimate right to use his credit cards. I informed the officer that I never received separation papers and showed them the text message where he authorized my use. Both officer immediately understood the situation and advised me to get a lawyer and to continue documenting everything. They left without pursuing charges.

What was absolutely unbelievable throughout all of this was that Todd had been telling the children that he'd take me back. But I had to call and ask him to come home. The kids loved their father but they were adamantly opposed to our reconciliation. I was too so I hired a lawyer and started divorce proceedings. Todd contested nothing and the alimony and child support award was more than enough to help make ends meet. So I did something for me. I enrolled in an online university. For over fifteen years, I had subjected myself and the kids to abuse so I could live the lifestyle I was accustomed. It had never occurred to me that I could have built that lifestyle on my own.

The *Un*-Relationship

The Un-Relationship Book is the title of my second published work. I chose the title because the negative prefix un means *to change or undo, not, reverse action, to deprive of, release from, opposite of, and contrary to* and is usually attached to such adjectives as *un*able, *un*clean, *un*equal, *un*safe, *un*happy, etc. In many relationships people seek to *"change or undo"* what has been done in the relationship; often times leading to divorce. We seek to *"reverse the action"* because we're feeling *"deprived"* in our relationships, therefore we want *"release from"* this thing (marriage or relationship) that has us bound. I have witnessed in my own marriages, the pain of being unequally yoked because we were the direct *"opposite of"* and *"contrary to"* one another.

As a teen and a young woman, I never wanted to be single. I dreamt of my wedding day and being married to the perfect man. I soon came to realize there is no such thing as a perfect man. In fact, there is no perfect person period! As young girls, we dream of the wedding dress, the church, and the family and friends attending our big day. We dream a fairy tale. A real marriage is full of ups and downs, submissions, and compromise.

In a God-ordained marriage, both the husband and wife are called to be submissive. The husband is called to submit and position himself underneath the authority of, or below God. The wife is then called to submit to the God Spirit in her husband. If the man allows himself to be led by The Most High and the woman is following the man's lead, that marriage is usually in perfect harmony with God's plan.

In reality, every marriage has its share of ups and downs, and spiritually--filled men and women who understand the covenant of marriage know that there must be some compromise. In marriage many times you may have to give up your right for someone else's wrong.

It's better to be at peace than to always be right. We hear people say marriage should be 50/50. This statement could not be further from the truth. Marriage takes 100% from both partners. The goal of marriage, according to Genesis 2:18, is for fellowship, companionship and mutual help and comfort. If each person is focused on fulfilling the needs of the other, it is most likely a happy union. Marriage is not for selfish people, and because of this, each person should be constantly thinking of the greater good of the relationship and not their own agenda.

The reason I wrote my books and participated in this anthology is so I can share my experiences to help people *change, undo, reverse the action of, and be released from* unhealthy habits and relationships. I'm not an expert on marriage and I'm certainly not perfect, but I was pretty good at getting things wrong. I was not being led by the God in me because I didn't allow the spirit to lead. By doing it wrong, I found that the best way to succeed at marriage was to submit to the leadership and guidance of God. The difference between a healthy marriage and an *un*healthy marriage is God holding the entire thing together. A husband and wife in tune with the God inside of them make a strong marriage. An *un*godly relationship is an *Un*-Relationship. It is the total opposite of or is contrary to the marriage or relationship The Creator has designed for us.

    I have been married twice. The first time I got married, it was not for love. I had known my first husband since we were children; we grew up in church together and he was the father of my twin boys. One day, I woke up and realized that I was the only single woman in my circle. I married him because of the boys and the self-inflicted peer pressure. We were married only one month before the *un*thinkable occurred. My husband, intoxicated and high on drugs, punched me in my face. I felt his wedding ring cut my eye. After several more punches, he started choking me until I blacked out. When I came to, I noticed my husband had taken the keys from my purse and drove off in my car. Our twins were just babies at the time, but my daughters witnessed the entire incident. There was blood all over the bedroom floor and bed. I put my hand to my face and there was even more blood. I can remember looking toward the doorway to the bedroom as he punched me and seeing my daughters jump up and down with their mouths open; I couldn't hear anything. I will never forget the deafening pain I saw in my children's eyes that night.

When my husband came back home after a couple of days, he was awakened by the police who had been watching the house and awaiting his return. A year went by before my husband would go to trial for the domestic violence case against me. We stayed married and during the entire time and I endured more abuse. He put his elbow in my throat, cut buttons off of brand new pajamas that were given to me as a Christmas gift from my grandmother, and even threatened to kill me. When he threatened my life, he told me, "this time your children are not here to save you." Eventually, his case went to trial and he was found guilty and served two years in prison for domestic violence, impeding a 911 call and cruelty to children. I stayed with my husband as he served his time because I was afraid of being seen as a failure. Several people had warned me about him before we got married, but I didn't listen because I didn't want to be the only *un*married friend and sister. When he was released from prison, he came back home to us, but I saw that he had not changed despite all of the cries, pleas, and lies he told from prison. When I noticed that my daughter had once again started sleeping with the phone under her pillow, I filed for divorce and never looked back. Our safety and my life were more important than being seen as a failure.

    I sought to *un*do the *un*wise decision to marry someone I didn't love; the second time my decision to marry was totally because of love. Wayne and I lived in the same neighborhood and graduated high school together, and I had been in love with him since the age of 14. As teens, we never dated, but we would talk on the phone sometimes. After we graduated, he went into the army and I remained good friends with his younger sister who always gave me the scoop on him. When Wayne returned home from the army (and after fighting in Desert Storm), we hooked up. He moved in with me and my three children and we eventually married. My husband always had an *un*healthy relationship with alcohol; even as a teenager he would come to my house with a carload of friends and they would leave beer cans and bottles in front of our house. As you can probably gather, we had a pretty *un*healthy relationship because of his drinking.

    Before Wayne and I married, we would get together, breakup, get back together, and break up again. The very last breakup as boyfriend and girlfriend lasted for almost 10 years. It was during this break up that I married my first husband. One day, after I was divorced from my first husband, Wayne contacted me through one of his family members and we started dating again and then, of course, he moved back in. I saw all of the red flags that caused our previous splits but I chose to ignore them. "He will change once we get married because he loves me just that much," I repeated to myself. Of course, loving me didn't change anything. As a matter of fact, I began to see some *un*familiar and *un*usual behavior and called his aunt to talk about it. His aunt's exact words were, "I hope that boy is not back on that stuff." "What stuff?" I asked to myself and to her. Apparently, during our years apart, Wayne had developed a drug habit. I tried for five years to love my husband through the addiction. I put up with buying cars only to have him trade them for drugs. I dealt with him obtaining good jobs and quickly losing them due to his abuse. Plus, whenever he got paid, Wayne would go on binges for days at a time so I also worried for his safety and health constantly.

    Despite all of it, I loved this man; hell, I had been in love with him for most of my life. From the age of 14 until this very day, I love him. I just couldn't deal with the drugs and the inconsistency that came with it. I remember filing for divorce on our very first wedding anniversary. We didn't divorce then, but that would not be the last time I filed but was *una*ble to follow through. I filed three more times before finally parting ways with the love of my life. When we divorced, he left the house we bought together, but we spent months trying to reconcile. Even though I was glad he left the house because I had peace, we went on dates and even sought counseling because I truly loved him. During one session with our pastor and first lady, I was asked this question, "if Wayne never changed and continued to be the person he is right now, could you see yourself with him for the rest of your life?" My answer to that question was a definite no. I did not want to be trapped in misery for the rest of my life.

    The love was *un*deniable, yes, but marriage to him came with a lot of emotional abuse. There were a few incidents of physical abuse, but overall, it was mostly emotional and verbal I think, in large part, due to his insecurity. Being an alcoholic and drug addict had a lot to do with it. We never went to any of our class functions because of his shame and desire to hide his problem from friends. Plus, Wayne knew there would be alcohol and when he drank, he always lost control. If I wanted to go without him, I was accused of going in an effort to see one of my ex-boyfriends. As a result, I never really went anywhere except for work, church, and date nights with him. When I was at work, he would call my phone the moment it was time for me to leave. If I didn't answer, he would ring it incessantly until I answered. I would then be interrogated as to whether I truly went to work or if I was off with a boyfriend. No boyfriend ever existed.

    In my first marriage, I was physically and verbally abused and had very low self-esteem because of it. In my second marriage, although we truly loved each other; I still endured emotional and verbal abuse; I wasn't happy in either union. No marriage should be a game of "survival of the fittest" and no spouse should live each day merely existing. I knew this but I didn't understand why I was attracted to men who abused me and suffered from alcohol and drug addictions. Even back then, if I sat down and wrote a list of qualities I wanted in a mate, neither ex-husband would fit the bill and it left me perplexed. But after years of soul searching and studying, I realized I wasn't necessarily attracted to them; they were attracted to me. As a healer, fixer, and empath, I have a sensitive nature and am extremely empathetic and sympathetic. Such characteristics are easily detected by addicts, abusers, narcissists, and psychopaths, who are experts at reading people and crafting a sob story to gain attention, sympathy, favor and second chances. I learned a valuable lesson with both men. Not only was I *un*able to repair them and *un*do the pain from their past, I was not their savior and it wasn't my responsibility to fix them.

While my first husband grew up in church, God was not in him. His mom was a very young mother of three boys and they all grew up watching her being physically abused. Wayne also witnessed his maternal grandfather beat his grandmother. and both his mother and grandfather were alcoholics. The apple didn't fall far from the tree. My second husband's parents separated when he was young and his mother was an alcoholic too. When he was a child, not only was she physically abusive to him when drunk, he was also witness to some despicable acts. He and his two siblings eventually moved out of their mother's house and lived with their dad. He never wanted to talk about his mom.

    My upbringing was nothing like theirs. Although my parents divorced when I was only three years old, I always maintained a relationship with my daddy. I was brought up in church and God lived in me, my mama and my daddy. My family was always in bible study or a prayer meeting when not in church service. My mama and grandmama kept me sheltered from a lot of things. Police were never called to our house for fights. I never knew about that type of violence until I became an adult. However, in retrospect, that may have been to my detriment because my children know it now.

Despite my upbringing and everything I learned from my parents and church, my marriages were the epitome of *Un*-Relationships. We were *un*equally yoked. I was *un*happy and *un*fulfilled. They were *un*kind, *un*holy and *un*well. While we had similar backgrounds in some areas, we were *un*like each other in those areas which were most important. With my first husband, I let the fear of being *un*wed influence the most important decision a woman can make for herself and her children. With my second husband, I *un*noticed warning signs because I truly loved him and believed he would change because he loved me too.

After reading this chapter, I hope you have insight into an *Un*-Relationship and understand what the Creator wants for you. Your desire and God's desire should be the same: to enter into a union where you're equally yoked. It is better to live in peace than to give yourself to someone who is *un*healthy. Breaking down the words Healthy Self, it also reads Heal-Thy-Self. You must be healed and whole to create that greater whole, and the two of you should complement, complete, supplement and enhance one another. By avoiding an *Un*-Relationship, you are ultimately avoiding divorce. The curse of divorce fell on me twice and I don't want to pass that curse to my children and I'm sure you don't either.

Disclaimer
Some of the context used in this chapter come from my book entitled, "The *Un*-Relationship Book: Getting Out of Your Own Way... Copyright 2016

Smoke And Mirrors And Marriage

It was the winter of 2006. I was at a popular night club with someone who I thought was my friend at the time, Renee. We were becoming aggravated because the guys there were becoming a nuisance. Unwilling to tolerate any more of their rude and tactless advances, we left and headed to my car. As we got in, a nice looking chocolate brother with pearly whites walked in front of my car and smiled. While I think he's checking for Renee, he was actually interested in hanging with me. After light conversation, he invited himself along with us. Renee and I were hungry and were headed to an all night spot for some chicken and mambo sauce. When Renee realized Hakeem would be tagging along, she asked to be dropped off first. I shrugged my shoulders. I didn't care. I was hungry and looking for to getting to know this fine brother.

Neither one of us is originally from the DC area, but

we're fully acclimated, loving mambo sauce and the other treasures the area has to offer. Our conversation is light and informal as I get up and go to the refrigerator for more drinks. Yes, I took him back to my crib. The wings and sauce are served in take-out spots, plus we seemed to hit it off immediately. Hakeem was not just fine, he was funny, intelligent and a hustler. I was already feeling him. The conversation took a serious turn when I asked, "how long have you been in the states and where is your green card?" He tells me he's been in the USA for a few years then reaches for his wallet and pulls out his green card. "Oh, okay," I thought. "He may just be a keeper." Fast forward nine months later and we're at the justice of the peace getting married. I have only one friend in attendance but his numerous friends and relatives flew from West Africa to witness the union. I should have known then that it was a mistake.

    The morning of my wedding, I'm crying and needed to speak with my best friend. She was living in Philly at the time and unable to support me in person. "Girl, I may be making a mistake because I keep crying and he's worried about his family and friends from Africa instead of paying attention to me." Bestie explains that Hakeem is just excited. It's his wedding day and his family flew from Africa. But she did advise me that if I was having doubts, not to do it. "You're right," I replied. I do love him. Maybe I'm just nervous." I dry my tears and make my way back to Hakeem and his family. We wait patiently for our turn to wed and once we were in front of the magistrate, everything went smoothly and I felt much better. Afterwards, we all went out to lunch and over the next few days, Hakeem and I showed them DC. They left and we started our life together.

    Eight months go by and everything is still going well. We're both working, saving money and building a good life when he comes home with red roses. Now, he's always been wonderful to me but he's never done that before. He asks me to sit down 'cause he needs to speak with me. He laid his wallet out and I'm wondering how much money he's about to give me when he pulls out his green card and makes his confession. "It's not real. I need you to sponsor me." Now I'm crying so badly everything becomes a blur. He grabs me, pulls me close and says, "I swear to Allah I didn't marry you just for this and I truly love you. Please stop crying." Infuriated, I push him off me and slap his ass so hard his eyes turned red from anger. Reaching for me as I turn to walk away, he says, "please, I beg you in the name of Allah. I love you. I just need for you to go through this immigration process with me." I stood there as he knelt at my feet begging for forgiveness and watched as tears streamed down his cheeks. I didn't know what to do or what to feel at that moment. My inner voice kept saying, "Lori, you're a damn fool." but another voice interjected, "you checked his green card. How could I know it was fake." What it boiled down to was the fact that he lied. But we're married now. I know he loves me as much as I love him. So I relent, let go of my hurt and agree to help him become a US citizen.

Four months later, we finally get an appointment for an Immigration interview. For some reason, our appointment is in Baltimore County and we were both nervous as we made the 45-minute trip. We were waiting for what felt like hours when finally my name was called. "Lori Peten," the officer continued to call me by my maiden name although I used my married name on all of the paperwork. "Lori Peten!" he called even louder and as I walked toward him, I was still wondering why he continued to call me by my maiden name. As soon as I stop in front of him, he stated sternly, "Lori Peten, you are under arrest for failure to pay a parking ticket."

Stunned, I reply, "you have got to be kidding me."

"No, ma'am."

A female officer approaches and says, "ma'am, I'm sorry. Would you like to call someone?"

"Yes. And can you ask my husband to come here?"

The officers researched the issue further and

explained that I didn't just need to pay the ticket, I was supposed to appear in court. Hakeem overheard it all and agreed to drive to Philly and pay the additional fees which had incurred since I didn't appear in court. Hakeem kissed me warmly and reassured that it was all going to be resolved quickly. As he left, I was escorted in a different direction by an officer. She led me out of the building, into an alleyway and protected my head as she helped me into the back of a squad car. All the while, handcuffed and crying with every emotion running through my mind and body. "Damn, this is fucked up!" I mumbled to myself as the officers took off. When we arrived at the station, a man sitting behind a small window processed my paperwork and another officer escorted me to this huge room with lots of bathrooms and ordered me to head to a molded stall and change. "And put your clothes and that wig in this bag." I was doing everything I could to not burst into tears and to not have to enter the stall and undress. But it couldn't be avoided so I obeyed.

Moments later, I'm out of my street clothes and into the standard correctional facility attire: cheap blue pants, shirt, and white tennis shoes. The C.O. leads me into another huge room with what looks to be about 50 beds. All of them were occupied except for eight...well, seven now. "Lawd have mercy!" I say to myself. "All the damn women...what in the world?" I claimed a bed by taking a seat on the mattress; it was as flimsy as a kindergartner's nap time cot. Frustrated, I glance around and make eye contact with some of the women. A few of them did a quick once over to check me out then laid back down on their bunk. "Ok, ladies! Lights out!" the C.O. yells and within seconds, all of the lights are dimmed. There was a dim glow from the bathroom area and as I fixed my eyes on a six inch crack in the ceiling, I laid down on the hard metal bed and placed both of my arms to my side as if I was in a coffin. The place looked, smelled and felt like death. After spending two nights in the raggedy jail, the C.O. finally called my name and told me to grab my linen. I couldn't get out of there fast enough.

I can't describe how quickly I grabbed that wrinkled plastic bag and scurried over to change into regular clothes. You probably would have thought I was Super Woman. Not even a goodbye, I throw open the door to freedom. The sun blinded me for a minute, but after I got used to it, I noticed there was no sign of my husband. Now I'm mad all over again. And just when I'm about to give up and conclude he's never going to show, he drove up, jumped out and explained that the police told him he wasn't allowed to park so he had to drive around the block to give me time to come out. Truth be told, though, I ended up waiting five minutes. But still...

"Paperwork. We have another appointment in 45 days."

"Oh no, we don't! I am through with Immigration!"

Hakeem knew what I had been through these last few days plus I'm sure he could tell I was tired, but he couldn't wait to drop the news. "Princess. We have another appointment in 45 days." I told him there was no way in hell I was going but he insisted. Irritated and worn, I laid my head back on the head rest and pretended to fall asleep. All the while, he kept begging "please" as we drove home via the Baltimore Washington Parkway. I refused to say one word and drifted off to sleep only to be awakened to Hakeem shaking my left thigh. "Baby, we really need to talk tomorrow. I need you to tell me what is the real reason you no longer want to go through this process with me. You are my wife and I expect you to finish what we started." Fortunately, he pulled up to our home so I didn't have time to respond. I rolled my eyes at him and rushed to get out of the car. I damn near broke my neck and busted my ass removing my clothes as I sprinted half naked through the living room to get to the shower. As the hot water poured down my body, I cried, contemplated, then cried some more. "Lord, please. I don't want to do it and see those folks again but he is my husband. Jesus, please tell me what to do!"

Saturday morning, I wake up and pull out every

bleach, Fabuloso, and Pine Sol bottle and get to cleaning while rehearsing what I am going to say to Hakeem. I heard the door unlock and by his posture, it was clear he was dirt tired. "Princess, I am really tired right now. I want to rest first but upon rising and supper, please be available for us to talk." Hakeem walks over to the safe and deposits more money into it. Then he walks towards me and kisses me on the forehead. I turn away but he can clearly see I'm upset. "Princess, this is the last time you will pull away from me when I try to show you affection. Do you understand me?" While I nod my head yes, I roll my eyes at him and he grabs my arms and asks again, "Do you understand me?" I lowly and slowly respond yes.

  Hakeem walks away and a few moments later, I hear the shower turn on then off and I see him proceed to our bedroom. I pour myself a glass of Zinfandel and open the balcony door to bring in the smell of fresh air. The house smelled mostly like Pine Sol and stew so I welcomed the breeze and I sat on the couch enjoying the

Spanish music blaring from outside. "Princess. Princess." I hear Hakeem whispering in my ear and I wake up. I look around and notice the food on the stove has been put in containers and a plate with a microwave cover is sitting out on the counter. Ignoring the fact that I'm still drowsy and upset, he starts in again. "Princess, I love you. I am not trying to bribe you but in order for us to get to the next level, I need for us to finish this process. If you don't want to and doubt me, I will pay you or give you whatever it is you like. I just need for us to get this done."

"Hakeem, this was the most embarrassing thing I ever had to go through. Being arrested at the Immigration Office is something I will never forget."

"Princess, you know they do a full background check on every applicant. It was a ticket and you didn't show up for court. So what? It's paid."

"But you weren't the one getting arrested; I was."

"Princess, let that go."

"I'm trying to but I can't. At least, not right now."

"Well, you're going to have to 'cause we got bigger things to deal with."

"Whatever."

"No, it's not whatever," he pops back.

"It is whatever."

"Princess, what can I do or say to prove I love you?"

"Hakeem, nothing, cause I just don't want to deal with this anymore."

"Princess, please don't give up on us. I want us to work and for us to move past this."

"I'm trying, but every time we get over one hurdle, another one is right behind it."

"Princess, I ask you. No, I beg you in the name of Allah to please continue with this process. We have a decent life; you want for nothing. Just figure out what it is you wanna do. Please, let's finish what we started."

"Hakeem, I want to trust you. But since early on, I have my doubts about you. You should have told me about the fake green card way before we got married. Now, I feel like our marriage was based on a lie."

"Princess, we have been married a while now. I don't give you any reason to doubt me. Please. I beg you."

"Okay," I agree reluctantly.

"Okay," he responds while handing me a one hundred dollar bill. "Go out, relax and have drinks on me. See you in the morning." I grab my cell phone and call my girlfriend to let her know it's party time.

Tuesday, Hakeem and I drive back to Baltimore County to meet with his attorney in order to discuss last minute questions and answers concerning the interview process. The lawyer explains because the arrest wasn't a felony, it wasn't going to delay our interview. The lawyer explained that the interview will consist of basic questions about our life such as where did we meet, etc. We give him his $500 deposit, say our goodbyes and stop for lunch. As we're waiting for our food, Hakeem asks, "do you know what type of business you want to open?"

"A cleaning business. But not homes."

"That would be good for you. I have been researching franchises and it's $1,200 down with equipment and a guaranteed contract at a $500 minimum. Go ahead and get busy and I will give you the funds."

"Okay, but I want to also learn more about the import business."

"Well, Princess, so both. I just want to see you happy." After grabbing our to go order, Hakeem turns to me and says, "Princess, I love you."

"I love you too."

It's the day of the interview, and after being sworn in, an officer asks, "Mrs. Obayomi, where did you meet your husband?" For hours, they continue to ask a series of personal questions regarding our relationship, relatives, and home life. Once I completed all of the questions, they ask me to step out. I pass Hakeem in the hallway and it's clear that he's nervous. I nod as if to say 'you got this' as he enters the room I just left. It took a total of four hours for the entire process and afterward, Hakeem, the attorney and I are standing in the parking garage discussing the matter. Hakeem's face is as red as a beet but he turns to me and lets me know I did well with the interview. Hakeem, on the other hand, stumbled through his words and asked the officers to repeat the same question several times. "It just didn't go well and I don't understand what happened. I was nervous," Hakeem spoke angrily. "But we are fine." As I stand there looking at him, tears are running down my face. And yet again, in that moment, I just knew something was terribly wrong. Despite his bad news and my uneasiness, I put in for my two weeks' notice and opened my commercial cleaning business. Life was good...or so I thought.

It was a stormy day as I race from my car to the mailbox. The letter from Immigration was the only thing there. Before opening it, I go inside and pour myself a glass of merlot. As I slowly open the thick envelope, I begin to read:

> We are informing you that your request has been denied. During our investigation, we came to the conclusion that your marriage is a scam. Hakeem has a wife in West Africa and she only went along with a divorce so she could eventually come to the US and reunite with Hakeem. Hakeem did not know the actual names of the company you worked for, where underwear was placed in the drawer, etc. There were three other bank accounts that Lori Obayomi clearly had no clue about in addition to a host of other discrepancies.

I read all six pages of the letter, fell to my knees and got an instant headache. When Hakeem walked through the door, I immediately jumped in his face, cursed him out and called him a fraud. After he asked me what I was talking about, I threw the letter at him, all the while cursing him out. He then backslaps me and ordered me to calm down and shut up. "Did this mother fucker just slap me!" For a moment, I stood still, shocked. "Yes, the fuck he did." I charged towards him and he flees to the bedroom and locks the door. "Nigga, you have said some foul, fucked up shit to me before but to put your hands on me is a fucking no-no. Bring your ass out here or I'm calling the cops!" As Hakeem opens the door, he snaps back, "first of all, lower your voice. And second, I and we are not in a fraudulent marriage. Now you sit your ass down and let's talk." "Fuck talking. Them papers say it all. I'm done talking to you." Hakeem grabs his keys and some cash and storms out.

    With him gone, I really go off. I throw shit and start rummaging through all of his paperwork looking for financial statements. And that's when it hits me. His ex-wife is in on the scam and is awaiting his green card so he can divorce me and bring his family to the States. "Lord have mercy! What am I going to do? I have made the biggest mistake of my life. Am I going through this because of the things I've done in my past? Karma is a bitch." As I sat looking around at the mess, my mind raced with thoughts. "How am I going to get out of this marriage? I cannot go to hell. What are my parents going to think? I have done some messed up shit but this...this is the ultimate." I couldn't stop thinking about going to hell. It consumed me along with the dread of going through another divorce. For two days, I barricaded myself in the house and spoke to no one until finally, I got an idea. I grabbed a bottle of water and one at a time, swallowed six Aleve pills.

I woke up the next day sick to my stomach and threw up everything from the night before. I was angry that I woke up. Looking at the clock, I realized I had more than enough rest and it was time to get my ass in gear and go to church. After a beautiful sermon, the pastor added, "when you lay down tonight and before waking up, you will have your answer. My heart raced when he spoke those words and deep down I truly believed what he said to be true. When they invited the congregation to altar call, I jumped out of my seat so I could get some of the blessed oil on top of my head. Maneuvering, I made my way a few feet from the steps as the pastor was walking down them and he said, "bless you, my sister" as he poured oil from a small jar. Satisfied, I made my way out of the sanctuary and stopped to buy the CD for today's sermon before driving home. When I opened the door, I noticed my husband still had not returned. Picking up my cell phone, I dial his number and when he answers, ask, "Are you ever coming back here?"

"Yes. I will be back later. Right now, I am working. I need to hire another attorney."

"Umhmm." I hang up the phone.

Although I'm mentally drained, my spirit is full after attending church and hearing such a moving sermon. Drifting off to sleep, I dreamt my bedroom was full of roses and the pastor sat at the end of the bed and spoke to me. "I told you that you would get the answer before you wake up and I want to tell you, you had no business getting married. You were not equally yoked and I did not join you two together. You did that on your own. So go on with your life. All is forgiven." I woke up confused. Sure, it was a dream but it felt real. Nonetheless, I got my answer and hightailed it back to North Carolina to get my life in order.

What I learned from this experience is that you can never know everything about someone and there are some things which we knowingly turn a blind eye. Best believe, I know check finances, credit scores, divorces papers and I ask tons of questions. I went through this screening process with everyone I dated and found someone I believe is trustworthy. We are in a loving, long term relationship and are taking things slowly. I will never settle nor look for love in all the wrong places.

As far as Hakeem is concerned, I filed for divorce and the paperwork was served to one of his previous addresses. He never responded so the divorce through went smoothly. The last I heard of him, he had managed to evade Immigration authorities and was residing in Iceland.

I Ain't Sayin She A Gold Digger...

I married for money and learned the hard way that money isn't everything. I'm being serious. Since social media and Instagram specifically, women flaunt their bodies and DM ball players and entertainers hoping to get broke off. And they've been called out by Kanye, Chris Brown, Charlie Puth and some have even been sued for it. When American Apparel's casting agency writes "Instagram Hoes and THOTS Not Welcomed," you know it's bad. I'm not judging anyone for what they feel they gotta do. To share a bit about my background, I am a former stripper and escort. My past influenced my decision to marry for money because I found myself wanting to be treated like royalty in a materialistic way. Since the whole ordeal, I grew out of that mentality. I know we as women like to have someone shower us with lavish gifts and pay our bills, but by the end of my story, you will understand why I am now happy to pay my own rent.

When I met my now ex-spouse, Stephanie, I was going through a break up with the woman I consider to be the love of my life, Tiny. At first, Tiny was my co-worker and we developed a very strong friendship and bond. We eventually took it to the next level and started sleeping together. From that moment on, we literally became inseparable. The only thing wrong with our relationship was that she was not ready to commit to me. It was like she was completely satisfied being friends with benefits. I felt like I was too grown to settle for that so I didn't agree with her friends with benefits arrangement at all. No matter how hard I tried to convince her that we should be together the maturity for wanting to be in a relationship with me just was not there. I finally came to the realization that our relationship wasn't going anywhere after two years passed by and we were no further along or better off. Tiny would come over on weekends we would get high, drink, and sex all night but when she would leave, I would feel a void. I was in a bad depressed place, and as hard as it was, I knew what I had to do. I had to cut her off cold turkey. I stopped all communication with her; we weren't even friends. We had a big blow up during a romantic getaway that led to this decision. So, even when I was at work, I would act like she wasn't there. I valued myself more than Tiny valued me. It hurt but I had to do what was right for me.

My daughter used to always play with the little boy next door, and as it turned out, and I was unaware that his grandmother Stephanie was openly gay and had been watching me for months. One day, Stephanie caught up with me as I was going downstairs and struck up a conversation about my tattoos. Then she mentioned that she liked that I always wore dresses and heels and my hair and makeup were always done. She was 19 years older than me and she seemed nice enough so I entertained her, especially since she mentioned being impressed by me. Although we didn't exchange numbers that day, she invited me to a barbeque at her daughter's house the following week. I ended up going and that was when and I exchanged numbers. We hit it off immediately, and for the first week, ended up talking all the time. Also, she lived close to my job so she would stop by and take me out to lunch. And, after knowing each other for only three days, she bought me some Christian Louboutin Red Bottom heels. I thought Stephanie was cool; I wasn't in love with her because it was way too soon for that but she impressed me and she took my mind off my last relationship.

    Before long, she really began to pique my interest when she began buying me any and everything I wanted. This included frequently sending flowers to my job. I knew it got under Tiny's skin when she saw them delivered and in my mind, I was enjoying the attention, gifts and making Tiny jealous. Then she started paying my rent and car note and even said that she wanted to marry me. Don't get me wrong, I had my own place, car, and money in the bank but I liked what she had to offer because it allowed me to just sit on the money I worked hard for without spending it. Now, the whole time she was courting me, I was in love with my ex. A part of me went along with all this because I just wanted to show Tiny a lesson about not taking me seriously. Even though I wasn't ready for marriage and did not love Stephanie, I got married just to make Tiny jealous and to not fall into the never being married curse. Stephanie and I married less than three months of knowing each other. I gave up my apartment and moved in with her full-time.

Stephanie's niece and daughter hated me. They thought I was being a gold digger because of the money she was spending on me. And because I used to be a stripper. In a sense, I guess I was. The way I saw it was that we had a mutual agreement. Before we got married, it was understood that she would pay all the bills and I would live my life as a live-in Barbie doll. She gave me a weekly allowance in addition to paying the household, medical and dental bills and helping buy stuff for my kids. Life was great. I was saving money and because I had no bills to pay, I bought myself a brand new Chrysler Three Hundred. It was like being married to an old woman was my second job.

    For some reason, though, things shifted fast. After only a month, she became evil. She had hit a rough patch in her business and was resentful towards me. She felt like I was coming up in the world especially because I had bought a brand new car and her car wasn't new. She complained that the entire marriage was about her taking care of me and I wasn't even offering to help her out. She started to lecture me that marriage is about partnership and not about me getting everything I wanted. I reminded her of our agreement but she tried to backtrack and say she did not mean for us to have an Anna Nicole Smith type of arrangement. She proceeded to say that she got married because she wanted a partner and she wasn't feeling that vibe from me. Then gradually, she stopped paying for things and cut off my allowance. When she stopped paying my car note, I was done. She did continue to pay the rent and electric bill because they were in her name.

As things were becoming more and more strained with my wife, Tiny had started to come around and wanted to be back in my life. She had changed and seemed more mature once she realized she lost me to a marriage so we started talking and hanging out again. I missed my ex so much. There were so many things that Tiny did for me emotionally that my wife did not do. I started to view my marriage as an obstacle standing in the way of my true destiny. Things at home were more and more strained with my wife. Stephanie and I were not talking and when we would talk, we would get very hostile towards one another. It got so bad that one day, at a shopping center, Stephanie and I fell out so badly over a difference of opinion that it turned physical and she left me stranded in the mall on my lunch break. I had to call my boss to pick me up. When

I got back to work I learned my wife had called the job and spoke with my boss to see if I got back to work okay. She used that situation to develop an alliance and friendship with my boss. Stephanie began talking about me to my boss in an effort to make me look badly. My boss didn't fall for it because of my work ethic and the fact that I've been seen in a positive light but it still made me mad.

    I didn't think it was possible, but things at home went from bad to worse. When I would get home from work, Stephanie would physically assault me in front of my kids. She took every opportunity to belittle and make me feel uncomfortable. She even served me with a three-day eviction notice, stating she wanted me and my kids out of her house. She locked me out of the house one day so that I couldn't get my stuff and the police had to be called. When they arrived, they advised her that, by law, she could not lock me out of the house. I was able to go back in but I didn't want to be there anymore. She had gotten even pettier and said she did not want me and my kids to touch anything she bought from the grocery store, including her laundry soap.

It wasn't long after all that that I started cheating on her with Tiny and making arrangements to get my own place and leaving for good. Tiny and I talked all the time and came up with a plan for me to leave and be with her. I no longer slept in the master bedroom and refused to be intimate with her. There were times when she tried but I would say mean stuff like, "eww" and "get away from me." One reason I didn't want her was that I was already involved in a sexual relationship with my Tiny so there was no reason for me to have sex with her. But the biggest reason simply was that the attraction was not there. I felt like she was a liar. She had really told me that she would take care of me and then flipped the script. Not only did she stop paying the bills, but she was physically violent and emotionally abusive to me in front of my kids. I understand this was an unconventional relationship, but I have always been a woman of my word so I took her at her word. If she would have been upfront with what she expected out of me things would have been different. I lost all respect for her so I was done.

I finally found my own place and moved out. Even on moving day, Stephanie was disrespectful and rude. She tipped the movers twenty dollars each and thanked them for getting the "trash" out of her house. My final words to her were, "I never loved you anyway." When I was finally settled into my new apartment, I had never felt so rejuvenated. I am currently in a loving and healthy relationship with my girlfriend Tiny. I immediately filed for divorce and because Stephanie did not contest it, it went through smoothly. But, from what I understand, Stephanie has still not gotten over it even though Tiny and I look back and laugh about the whole situation. Stephanie is still calling people and asking about my whereabouts but I will never talk to her again. She just won't get the message.

A valuable lesson that I want all women to learn from my story is to not marry for money unless love is truly involved. Money is great to buy things but those things will never make you happy. And it sure can't help you be happy with someone you don't love. What good is someone doing so much for you if at the end of it all you wind up miserable and they try to take it all back from you anyway? It wasn't that I didn't like my spouse (in the beginning), but to this day I realize I just didn't have the level of love needed for a marriage. I am a strong and intelligent woman, so everything that my ex-wife did for me I am more than capable of doing for myself and I am currently building my empire. Sadly, though, I let greed cloud my judgment.

Lessons From The Other Side

*****

Sure, it would be grand if all the snakes in our lives hissed or were marked by nature with certain warning colors or physiological shaping. In many instances, snakes are camouflaged in the garbs of money, position, material possessions, education, power, physical appeal, gifts and talents, ministry and even in personal brokenness. The snake attracts us, scaling our eyes and senses to the precarious dance with a viper whose kiss can be a deadly, hooked bite.

*****

My ex-husband and I met while in college. He was a popular and very attractive fraternity guy who exuded a charm, handsomeness, and sex appeal that hot-glued the scales over my eyes. I was an expected and on the path to becoming a "success story" -- a college student leader, sorority woman, honors program, Pre-Med, community-oriented, pretty and intelligent. (Yes, intelligent, even though I had a messy start to the marriage thing. Don't judge me.) But, I was trying to find my purpose outside of other people's expectations. My future did not seem to have the same myopic focus that others had of it. I was doing what was expected of me but my own life design expectation blurred. Like a print in a darkroom, the image was developing.

He was a ladies' man and I was the lady for the season, much to the chagrin of his sorority sisters and a few other ladies within Black Greekdom. I was the one that snagged "that guy." And, I was all too proud that I did it. I tried to love him the best way that a 21-year old woman craving a level of significance that seems to elude her could.

*****

Often, it is not the snake that will kill you. It's the poison that courses through your body that does the damage.

*****

Who arrives late for her courthouse nuptials and leaves the groom standing at the altar...well...Clerk's office? The signs were there for both of us. I did not want to be late to my own nuptials. Honestly, I didn't. Yet, I found myself in over 2 hours of traffic for what should have been a forty-minute drive over the bridge and on the road. I felt horrible as I watched the courthouse doors close. Was that a sign?

In full transparency, I did not miss the signs but decided to not heed them. God and my guardian angels were working overtime throwing a hint here, a remark over there, a random call from an ex-boyfriend, a prophetic word, a scripture, and of course, a traffic tie-up that seemed literally like every... single...car...tractor... bike...traffic signal...all stopped at the exact same time! But, undeterred and completely depleted, I apologized, cried and pleaded with my now ex-husband that I was not trying to stand him up at the alter... I mean City Clerk's office/desk. I did love the man. He had endearing moments and we enjoyed fun times together. In fact, whenever a commercial for the Titanic® movie comes across the screen, I chuckle. One of our first dates was a showing of the movie and there were waterworks...from him! It was a great memory. On that winter's night, everything felt warm, comfortable, and safe. He was a human in search of love and meaning. I, the same. Fast forward, six months later and in a fury of calls, I found a minister, said "I do" and got married two days after our calamitous courthouse scene. All around craziness and never a good idea.

*****

There is a Bible verse in the book of Proverbs that sums it up: "Pride goeth before destruction, and a haughty spirit before a fall."

*****

    The start of the nuptials was pigsty messy. My short-lived marriage had heaps of freshly dug dirt raining down on me... and the illustrative language was near physical reality and the basis for an almost Lazarus style resurrection that God did in my life. From time to time, I reflect on the bruised ribs, black and blue marks on my body, patches of hair that broke off from the stress, and the infant son whose beautiful sweet face needed me. Many times, we know we are petting a snake. There may have been signals that danger lurked. Perhaps we believe that our snake would never strike or it's slow but increasing constriction suffocated our lives, unfortunately, and literally. Through the divorce process and years' long healing process, I understood snakes are not always people.

Often, divorce forces situations and engagements that people are neither prepared for, in the best interests of the children nor the other party because level-setting, internal work must happen first. If there was any time in my life that felt like I shackled myself to one of Satan's minions who was determined to make my life a living hell (since I granted permission with "I do"), the almost two-year process of divorce and constant panic attacks would qualify as my personal Dante's inferno. With the scales ripped from my eyes, I wonder what did I do to my life!

Divorce, fueled by anger, hurt, sadness, grief, control, manipulation, and power issues (to name a few), must be addressed and everyone needs to be empowered to be better and healthy. It's not solely trying to communicate with the other party or a workshop on co-parenting. Such a class may be a resource but when SUBTERRANEAN levels of damage have been done, it's not enough. If control, manipulation, and power issues that continue, abuse needs to end and all parties need to be empowered to be better and healthy. Real talk: If you are trying to move forward with your life, seeking a deeper sense of self, fine-tuning your gears to be better and more wholesome, and your former partner goes out and gets a tattoo saying: "Witches Bow to Men", "Thuggish" or "Pimping Ain't Easy", or flagrantly flaunts the sin of their adultery and companion, and/or their lifestyle choices continue to be suspect, you must establish appropriate boundaries...in love. And, that means you must love yourself enough to protect your neck. Some snakes are so dangerous that they need to be in a fully contained space and away from you. Period.

*****

Perhaps, this a good point to mention that snakes do not have to be an ex-partner but relationships and thoughts that no longer serve you and who God is calling you to be.

*****

During the divorce, I had a friend who did not miss a moment to use the exact words or some derivative of "God won't bless no mess" with the authority of a sanctimonious bishop. In this season of my faith formation, I was challenged greatly in reconciling that: 1) this situation was not what I hoped for and was a muddle of pain and conflict; 2) God was gravely disappointed in me for not deciding to not pursue this marriage and I deserved the abuse of the divorce process; 3) there is a small child....a baby...that was produced in the union and he was a blessing; and 4) perhaps, both grace and blessing were not mine to have (excluding the blessing of my son).

*****

But let me tell you what I know to be true: God blessed me despite my mess!

*****

"Wait, what?! Stephanie, what are you talking about?" It's clear that your marriage started messily. Your relationship before you got married may have had some mess that you aren't discussing. And, girl, you may have been a mess yourself. So...yeah, God don't bless no mess!"

Now that this is all out of someone's system, let me share what I learned in my process of healing. When I returned to my mother's home, I was battered, bruised and broken. I felt like a failure. I was victimized and treated horribly in my deepest physical and emotional pain. There were things done and said that cut me to the bone. The divorce process and exchanges with my ex-spouse were contentious and vicious. I battled depression and anxiety behind a masked smile. As clear as streak-free glass: God can and will bless you despite, because of, in your mud pie-making clothes, "life's a shamble", off-track life.

I could go on and one about the grace and blessings that I experienced during and since that time. My "blessings" were a direct result of God's grace. I did not have or act in any way that should have afforded me that blessing. For example, my first full-time job post separation was a temporary position at a Wall Street investment bank that opened into a full-time role. I did not know there was an open position. Quite frankly, I did not think that I would qualify for the position. But, grace.

The Greek entomology for the term we use "blessing" or "blessed" is makários "(from mak-, "become long, large") – properly, when God extends His benefits (the advantages He confers); blessed."[i] An alternate and corollary translation is "happy." The word, grace, is derived from the Greek word "Charis". Theologians address the meaning of the word 'Godly kindness' for those whose sin has deemed them the most contemptible, loathsome and shameful of persons.

Often, God's grace is described as a gift you (really) didn't deserve. God doesn't give His grace by measuring our goodness (and because of sin, we really aren't all that wonderful). Do you remember the "gold" star board in elementary school? When a student did "good work", they or the teacher would put up a star. Thank God, grace is not given by merit or works: It is given out because of His love for us.

As I look back at my journey through divorce (and life, quite frankly), I recognized the contextual application of "God don't bless no mess" misaligned with my experiences. God blessed me in my mess. I did not say my mud-stained clothes did not exist. However, I learned lessons on the grace of God and extending grace to myself. The divorce process was far from pleasant and "happy" as the adjective is often and superficially applied, but I could find a joy and peace that truly surpassed understanding. Absolutely, I removed myself from relationships and thoughts that did not serve me and/or could go where God was taking me. To describe the outcome of it: What freedom!

*****

Neither divorce nor my ex-spouse was the snake. Both were elements of the poison and constriction.

*****

I don't regret the marriage. My greatest earthly love is a product of our union. Second, I had to learn to find self-love, significance, and value outside of the prescribed expectations of others and myself and unearth it in God. Of course, the marriage failed. I failed. "Stephanie, you shouldn't consider yourself a failure. You had some real challenges. You were young. You tried."

Yes, and failed.

I am comfortable acknowledging my failed marriage. I wish that I could say that the pieces came together, dusted off and were spit shined. They weren't. Instead, the grim task of burying the young woman who was poised to be a "success story" was mine alone. I eulogized her short life and stepped back from the gravesite with memories of who she was and a commitment to never forget her. A remarkable part of my personality, personhood, and perspective —my "Who am I?" necrotized. Like a booby-trapped and heavily mined parcel of land, the divorce process detonated my life. Around my heart and soul were the remains of a person I once knew. She was an awesome beauty who did not fully see nor could appreciate herself outside of the challenges of life. I loved her, struggles and all.

The illusion of life that we create for ourselves vested in superficial and/or temporal things can be snakes. Our snake can charm us to believe that the

5,000-square foot house, luxury car, designer apparel, and 2.5 kids are evidence of our lives being together; impervious to a snake bite. Perhaps, we did not "end up" like our mother, father, sister, brother, aunt, uncle or cousin because we don't have their demons, live in the hood, struggle like they did/do, and we are somehow bite-proof. Maybe, you and/or your ex (or soon-to-be "throw up the deuces" partner) are college educated, esteemed in the social circles of life, sit or stand in the pulpit on Sunday mornings, or raise a hand during worship because the Spirit is moving and the snake's hissing is distorting your hearing.

Recognizing there is a host of reasons behind the marriage failure and divorce, I decided to examine myself, the situation and related circumstances and established better thought processes and actions. I do things differently and better. I am incredibly far from and will never achieve perfection. Perfection was never the goal.

*****

Many times, snake handlers die.

*****

Divorce sucks! Until it does not. Faith and ministry folks will jump up and talk about the sanctity of marriage. Agreed, I believe that to be true. I also believe that God desires us to be in healthy and affirming relationships and marriage. God doesn't want us to perish, either. I will never condone a message to stay in a marriage where your physical, emotional, mental and/or spiritual health is in jeopardy. God is bigger than divorce and its pressures and challenges.

*****

Once bitten, twice shy.

*****

Perhaps, your future will include remarriage. Or, it may not. For a long time, I struggled with the idea of marriage again. Although I did not have the tools and life experiences in my first marriage, I was deeply disappointed that it failed. As sophomoric or naive as it may seem, Bill and Claire Huxtable were weekly reminders of what marriage and family could be. And, it did not work out that way; some reasons were his, some were mine.

*****

It took me a long time to be open to remarriage. I had relationships that seemed on track to wedding bells and did not (and that's completely OK).

*****

At times, I felt ambivalent towards remarriage. If it happened, "Amen." Let it be who God desired for me and that I am who God desired for me to be should I embark on this leg of the journey. If not, I am still whole and complete. The title and role of wife or spouse did not define me as a woman or person. Moreover, I would not let an individual, institution, society or my own wrong thinking advise me otherwise. What I know to be true is the divorce experience and the healing journey has prepared me to be better in my next marriage.

And, look... I'm scarred. Very tender places remain that the slightest pressure or touch may elicit tears. Those spaces may never be what it once was but I am able to shield and not expose it. During the 365 days of the year, inevitably something brushes against and hurts it. I understand why and can communicate what the pain is and be better at protecting the injury while giving its time to heal to the best of its ability. More often than not, I do not expose myself to people or things that will elicit discomfort, anxiety, or pain. When I am unable to steer clear of or must engage certain situations, I am better equipped to navigate it. Surprisingly, sometimes those pain points no longer hurt.

*****

Final Note

*****

A few years ago, I was watching a cooking show and the guest (a pastor) was discussing using items of food that others would discard to make great meals. Then he made a statement that has and will continue to travel on my life's journey. Here it is: "Everything in the hands of God is useful."

*****

To be clear: Divorce is included in "everything." Full stop.

*****

In Psalms 13: 1-2, David cried out "How long, O LORD? Will you forget me forever? How long will you hide your face from me? How long must I wrestle with my thoughts and every day have sorrow in my heart?" One cannot miss the anguish in David's words. It resonates because we, too, have cried out to God wondering if He has heard our cries as we labor along the journey. David has come to the end of himself (again). He had to meet a dead-end.

We may believe we have reached a dead end in Life. The dead end may be in relationships. We may struggle with the acceptance that not all earthly relationships, especially love relationships, are for a lifetime. We may struggle with loving someone and allowing the person to be who and what they are, even when it means they can no longer be a part of your life, in the same way, as you seek God for the things He has in store for you. It is the letting go of past things and coming to the end of ourselves so that God can freely move in our lives.

Coming to the end of our self is the "Dead End." It is where we meet God and His grace in a new and special way. It is the place where our faith must be stretched and grow. It is the place where we further our essential relationship with God. The Dead End is the place where God creates and shows us His road to travel.

Do you see the "Dead End" sign ahead? Are you standing next to it right now? This is wonderful news! Today, know that you have reached the end of yourself and the power that divorce sought to exert over you. For me, and I pray for you, divorce is the end of one thing and the space where to receive anti-venom and be loosed from the constriction. Divorce is the commencement point of a new level of the journey with God. Be free. Be healed. Stay well.

[i]Source: Bible Hub. 3107- Makarios, Greek. ☐
http://biblehub.com/greek/3107.htm

Things Aren't Always What They Seem

I met him at church. He had recently relocated to my hometown from Florida and was already an active member. He served on the security ministry and in addition to never missing a service, he could also be seen at Wednesday Bible Study. The single women considered him a catch but I wasn't shopping for a husband. I was focused on being a mother to a beautiful, teenage girl as well being promoted on my job. I'm unable to disclose for which government agency I work but it was my goal to secure a top secret clearance. So, like Jay-Z said, "I'm focused, man."

Even though the women pursued him, Mark chose to pursue me. For months, he'd go out of his way to speak and being a Christian woman, I replied but always kept it moving. Now don't get me wrong. I was focused, not blind. Mark was handsome, light skin, tall and had gorgeous green eyes. When he finally summoned the courage to ask me out, he suggested bringing my daughter Mia along. After explaining that wouldn't be necessary because I had family in the area, he changed our plans to a more adult venue. So I dropped Mia off with her aunt and we headed to a cozy little jazz spot outside of Washington, D.C. We soon discovered that we had similar interests and dreams and because we connected instantly, we were inseparable.

 Although I managed to spend as much free time with him as I could find, I still served in the church, studied for my promotion and made time for Mia. She had a beautiful voice and in addition to teen ministry, she also sang in the choir with her friends. Because of my military background, I enrolled her in her high school's Marine ROTC program and like I hoped, she loved it. I was proud to see my daughter following in my footsteps. Mark stepped in and volunteered to transport Mia to her activities on the days I had to work late. Her father was never a part of our lives and we were fine with it. Because I was so close to my parents, my dad filled that void with my mother helping alongside him. They'd been married for more than twenty years when a car accident took his life. That was in 2000. It's 2003 now and having Mark around made me realize how much I missed a man's presence. I had told him all about my father and he seemingly understood because he stepped up no questions asked. He was so attentive, gentle and considerate and he constantly poured into me and comforted me when I needed it most. I truly loved that man.

    The demand of my job increased drastically and Mark was there for me again. When I stayed late at work, Mark picked Mia up from school and drove her wherever she needed to go. While it seemed to be the perfect arrangement, Mia didn't seem happy and began to withdraw. No longer was she interested in participating in ROTC or choir. And while in church, she stopped singing and started to hang around a different crowd. The other members and I weren't too familiar with these kids; they were sullen. And if the rumors were correct, many of them were smoking weed or worse. We were certain some of them were secretly gay. Mia's transformation made absolutely no sense to me. Before she began hanging with them, she was a pretty, feminine girl who loved wearing dresses and heels. Why was she now wearing pants and dressing in all black? We got along so well, why was she now angry and defiant? There was one particular incident that seriously bothered me, but I had no idea what to do. I saw her racing out of our home and into her aunt's car, slamming the door. When I asked what's wrong, she shouted, "I'm not living in this house with him!" I turned towards the house and saw Mark standing in the doorway looking confused. *My heart sank.*

No way was I going to choose him over Mia so Mark and I really needed to talk. When I asked him for an explanation, he seemed to be confused too. We discussed it a bit and concluded she was probably jealous that she had to share me with someone else. That seemed to make the most sense. My parents were married all my life, and as an only child, I would have been jealous if anyone new injected themselves in our family dynamic. After this realization, I made it a point to spend more one-on-one time with Mia. I wanted to assure her that no one would ever come between us.

I spent more time with Mia and constantly reminded her that I'd always put her first, and she seemed to return back to her old self. So after dating only six months, Mark and I decided to get married. This was my first marriage and his third. Because we were in our thirties and got along so well, we didn't see the point in waiting. He was an excellent husband and stepfather although some of his behavior was a little odd. Mark would constantly call to ask my whereabouts and when I'd be coming home. And he even installed a GPS tracker app on my phone. He explained that because of my job, he was concerned for my safety. I was incredibly independent and didn't need to be looked after, and even though it was strange, I appreciated his concern. He'd also disappear for a couple of days without warning and when he returned, explained that he went to visit his mother. Infidelity never crossed my mind because other than that, he was always home. I just never understood why he wouldn't tell me beforehand. There was something else that was strange and no matter how many times he explained it, it just never felt right. That was his bedtime routine with Mia.

    The first time I learned of this, Mia was making her way upstairs to get ready for bed. Mark got up to follow her and when I asked why, he said, "to tuck her in." I went off and told him that would never happen, explaining that she was a 15-year-old girl and didn't need a grown ass man tucking her in. Mia remained quiet while Mark assured me it was OK; they had a bedtime routine. I looked at her, worried, but she didn't seem scared and she never said a word. So I reluctantly relented and watched suspiciously as they made their way upstairs. I waited a few moments then crept upstairs slowly, making sure the stairs didn't creak. *This nigga must think I'm stupid.* But, as I made my way down the hall and peeped around the corner into her bedroom, my suspicions were unconfirmed. Mia was laying in the bed, covers drawn over her as Mark read from a book. Yeah, it looked innocent enough but still, something didn't feel right.

All was finally revealed about six months after that incident. Mia had another meltdown, stormed out of the house and into her aunt's car. She was furious with Mark again and as a last resort, decided to move in with her aunt. She refused to be anywhere near him. She had her things packed in her aunt's car and neither had ever discussed this with me. And on top of my daughter suddenly moving out, Mark had disappeared again. I was home alone and utterly confused. I desperately wanted to fix things but I had no idea what was wrong. Then, a call from my mother revealed everything. Obviously shaken, my mom detailed exactly why Mia hated Mark; he had been sexually abusing her for months. I almost dropped the phone. I had certainly dropped the ball. I saw the signs but couldn't put two and two together. *Who would?* It just wasn't something I ever thought I'd go through...let alone Mia. I served in the military and was working to become an agent. I was trained to spot people like this. I just never believed it would hit so close to home.

As I recalled Mia's drastic personality change, I realized it first occurred during my courtship with Mark but I had figured it was because she was jealous that I was spending time with someone else. *Oh, how I wished that was the case!* Our relationship with lightning speed and he was always too eager to step in and look after Mia. He didn't just groom Mia, he groomed me too. The fact that he was so concerned with my whereabouts that he installed a GPS app should have been the kicker but his explanation made perfect sense. I truly believed he loved and was looking out for me. Because I failed to see the signs, my baby girl was raped and sodomized in my home and under my nose. And according to my mother, she no longer had any interest in boys; the sweet, feminine Mia I knew was gone. She was a lesbian now.

And Mark was nowhere to be found. While his disappearances were unexplainable before, it all made perfect sense now. He'd run away when he feared Mia told me about the abuse. He was right to be concerned. I had a department-issued weapon and was an excellent shot. When I hung up the phone with my mother, my first impulse was to put a hole in his head. I was shaking, crying and screaming. *Why the fuck did I let this monster into our lives?* Unsure what to do next, I managed to calm down enough to call a couple from the church. Married for decades, they were paired to mentor me and Mark through our new marriage. I'm thankful I called them; they were as shocked and appalled as I but they helped me view the situation logically. I needed to speak with my husband.

I called and texted Mark incessantly for days but

they all went unanswered. As I continued to search for him, I received a lot of criticism from family and friends. Even though Mark was away, Mia continued to live with her aunt and I made no moves to leave him and bring her home. They couldn't understand it. My family never considered me foolish or desperate for a man, but they called me that plus a lot worse. Mia wasn't angry and never criticized my decision; she was just disappointed and that hurt more than anything. However, I stood my ground and waited for him to return my calls.

When Mark finally called, my voice was sugary. I simply asked him to come home so we could talk. Never did I reveal what I knew so he was under the impression that he had overreacted by disappearing again. Once he arrived home though, I told him that Mia had revealed their secret. He was silent but nervous as I waited for an explanation. All he could do was apologize and I accepted every one of his apologies. I further explained that Mia would no longer be living with us, but if he wanted, he could remain here with me. I couldn't fathom sleeping with him, but I shared that eventually, I'd like us to move past this - I first needed an explanation.

For two weeks, we lived as husband and wife as he avoided explaining. The air was so thick with tension, we both felt it. Despite that, I still did everything I could to assure him that I was on his side...almost everything - I could not bring myself to sleep with him. One evening as we got ready for bed, we finally had the conversation that exposed it all.

My voice was calm, I spoke slowly and started, "I know you're afraid to tell me but I'll understand if it "just happened." She's 15. She started flirting a little and things got carried away, right?" His head hung low and he remained quiet. "If she was flirting and it went too far, I get it. I can forgive you." I got the feeling he wanted to speak, so I remained silent and waited for him to summon the courage to do so.

"Yeah. She came onto me. She started flirting first and

saying stuff and we got carried away. It only happened a couple of times. I'm so so sorry. I love you and I want you to forgive me. Please."

My voice was smooth as I uttered, "I forgive you. But what you did was against the law. I don't want you to go to jail. But my whole family knows and they want to lock you up. You need to write up a statement detailing everything you just told me."

"Yeah, yeah. I can do that."

I pushed a pen and pad towards him and he began writing down everything: how it started, when, where, and what he did to her. When he was finished, I looked it over to ensure its accuracy, ripped the confession from pad, folded it and slid it into my back pocket. I grabbed my phone from the other pocket and dialed 911. *That mother fucker thought I'd choose him over my child. He must have been out of his mind!*

    Mark made no attempt to run or attack me, so after the police arrived and took him away, I called my daughter. I explained that my church mentors helped me devise a plan. We wanted Mark to feel relaxed enough to give a written statement to the police. Once he signed it, we could press charges and have him convicted. In order for it to work, though, everyone had to believe I wanted to reconcile with Mark. They needed to feel and behave as if they were utterly disappointed in me. Only the couple from church and my boss knew the truth. I was almost sick with disgust just speaking to him but I was doing it for a good reason...her and every other young girl with whom he may come in contact. Mia needed to testify in order for him to serve jail time but she was too afraid to do so. Because she had kept a journal detailing her abuse, and his description of what occurred matched hers, the judge ordered that Mark be added to the Maryland sex registry list. It wasn't the win I was hoping for but I'm thankful he's out of our lives.

    Mark and I were legally separated but still attending the same church. Mia avoided him like the plague and I did too...until I noticed him attempting to move on with another member. By no coincidence, she was a mother to girls. One evening, I pulled her aside and warned her, even pulling his name up on the sex registry list. She thanked me profusely and immediately ended the relationship. He disappeared from church after that and I didn't see him again until years later. Happily married to my second husband, we ran into Mark at a grocery store. My husband being the man that he is, introduced himself and shook Mark's hand. A few moments later, a woman walked up to Mark and it was obvious they were an item. My instinct was to warn her, but he abruptly ended the conversation and took off in the other direction.

    I pray to God that she and every other woman out here do some sleuthing and check the names of these men against the sex offender's registry.

It Had To Happen

I married a stranger. He wasn't a stranger in the arranged marriage sense. I had known him since the eighth grade and while we weren't close friends, we traveled in the same circle. Upon graduation, we went our separate ways and I never saw him again until he walked into the strip club where I worked in 2000. After recognizing me, we forged a friendship. He would come through, talk to the girls, tip them very well and spend the rest of happy hour chatting with me. When he first asked me out, I declined. He seemed like such a sweet man, I really didn't believe he could handle me. At the time, I was a lot. Hell, I still am. But something told me this good boy could possibly take my life in a different direction. I wasn't ready for that since I made really good money as a dancer and truly believed it was where I belonged.

To say I was emotionally and spiritually damaged is

an understatement. I had been a victim of child sexual abuse since the age of five, so I never believed I could have a healthy relationship or that a decent man would ever want me. My body count was too high, i.e. I had slept with too many men. Exotic dancing could now be added to my resume. And even though I held a bachelor's degree, I was a cliche: an African-American single mother. Before I ever became a stripper, there were a few men who were considered a real catch and while they were okay sleeping with me, none of them would seriously date me. Coupled with the fact that I felt most at home working at the strip club, it was my belief that this was all God destined me to be.

Then I dated him. And he was perfect. I constantly told him so. He seemed annoyed when I said it but it was his lies that drew me to that conclusion. I realized later it was because he mirrored everything I said and did. He made me feel warm, protected and loved. Yes, there were signs and some arguments left me feeling confused and doubting his honesty. When I explained to my friends how he made me feel, they berated me for even complaining about him. He wasn't physically abusive and, as far as I knew, he wasn't cheating; I was been overly dramatic. It took some time, but when I was finally able to verbalize how he was making me feel, I explained it to him. He knew my history of abuse and I told him the way he spoke and argued reminded me of my abusers. He used the same tactics they implored to absolve themselves of guilt and put it all on me. The feeling was all too familiar and at times, I reverted back to that child victim, giving him what he wanted while making excuses for his mistreatment of me. In the beginning, he would make an effort to stop and we would have mature discussions when we disagreed. But he'd eventually revert back to his old pattern and I would become that scared little kid again. Just like that feeling of familiarity I felt when I first walked into a strip club, his behavior towards me sparked the same. I concluded, once again, that I didn't deserve any better and this would be my lot in life.

I settled for that behavior also because I didn't believe I would be nothing more than a promiscuous little girl and former stripper. I had internalized everything that had been done to me and still felt it was my fault, there was something about me that made men want to hurt me. So, despite my triggers, we moved in together after dating only one month. He didn't feel like a stranger because I convinced myself that knowing *of him* from middle school essentially meant I knew who he was as a man. Also, my daughter loved him and it felt good to have a consistent father figure in her life. When I started to push for marriage, he would push back saying we weren't ready but my overwhelming emotion truly believed we could make it work. We didn't have be rich to get married. He soon relented and we got married within a year of dating. Our wedding day was even the one-year anniversary of our first date, July 25, 2002. We immediately tried for a child and I got pregnant in December. That's when all of his lies came tumbling down.

To his defense, some of the deceit was simply due to his ignorance. He spent too much time feigning perfection that he failed to investigate some of the treachery going on in his own life. But when I discovered he wasn't who he said he was and the memories he shared with me were all fabricated, I was enraged. I couldn't fathom how he could marry me knowing all along he had been lying the entire time. I wasn't a Christian then, but I explicitly told him that marriage meant forever and I didn't want to be a single mother of two children. It was easy for me to believe him when he agreed that divorce was off the table. His parents have been married for more than 40 years.

So there it was. I was having a stranger's baby. I

had no idea who he was and it made me sick to my stomach. On top of the sickness and disgust, I felt cheated, hurt and angry. And trapped. Marriage was supposed to be forever but I was bound to share the rest of my days with a deceiver, a stranger. I wasn't given the option to choose if I really wanted *this guy*. If I had known who he really was and not the person he pretended to be, I never would have married him. I was cruel enough to tell him so on several occasions. So throughout the first half of our marriage, I made him pay. I was verbally vicious, threw things, hit him and constantly threatened to leave. In my heart, I knew I wasn't leaving because I honestly had nowhere to go. I couldn't afford two children on my own and even though I danced a few times while married, there was no way I was going to return to that life again. When I was cruel, he begged and pleaded for me to stay and did whatever he could to make it better. That was the during the first half of our marriage, though. The second half was entirely different.

During the second half of our marriage, there was a reckoning within me. In addition to fighting the same battles with him, I began to suffer from triggers and flashback due to the abuse. When I suggested counseling, he agreed but he did not stay long. I remained behind and did the work. I had to. My fury and anger had begun to affect our everyday lives. If I wasn't screaming at him, the kids or the dog, I was lying down for weeks in a depressed haze. As I began to read *The Courage To Heal* by Laura Davis and completed the workbook assignments, I realized that everything that was done to me wasn't my fault. I was groomed. And I was deserving of so much more than what was done to me as a child. As I explained this to him, I encouraged him to read the chapter dedicated to spouses of sexually abused victims. He never did. As a matter of fact, he did little to nothing at all. He went to work, came home, watched television and hardly pitched in around the house. I felt as if I was doing all the work, all the loving and he was just there to absorb it all. I wanted him to love me back. I just learned that I was deserving of it so it was something I craved from him.

    By this time, I had given my life to the Lord and took being a Christian seriously. There were stories of women in the Bible who were married off to men who didn't love them. The women remained obedient to God and their spouse even though they didn't feel the love in return. I felt like those wives from the Old Testament; I felt like Leah. So I persisted. I truly believed our marriage was ordained and that God would turn it around. Miracles arose from our mess of a marriage that easily led me to that conclusion: I healed from abuse, I gave my life to Christ and I was reunited with my father. It turned out that our church secretary attended a different church; one that my father ministered. I was reunited with him five days after we married and learned he lived just minutes from my in-laws and the house where I grew up. My grandmother lived in a house that was literally behind the strip club where I used to dance. Yet, I was reunited with them all after I married. How could this marriage not be ordained?

Counseling also helped me reconcile the deceit I felt from marrying a stranger. I told him and showed him that I forgave him. While I expected the forgiveness to change us, it changed me. I sought to display the characteristics of a Godly wife so my delivery was softer. I was more respectful, patient and a lot less hostile and aggressive. I focused on what I loved most about him and instead of criticizing or trying to fix him, I spoke life instead. I prayed for him, for us and our family. I found joy in every little thing and avoided arguments as much as possible. I thought I loved him in the beginning of our marriage, but I didn't. That was infatuation. To love someone is to accept them as they are, flaws and all. In the beginning of our marriage, I worked to change him. That's not how God loves us. He knows our hearts but loves us anyway. He sees our faults, our selfishness, and our mistakes and He continues to love us the same. His grace and mercy don't diminish when we do wrong. He loves us through it all.

After realizing this, I loved my husband even though he did nothing differently. He continued to disregard me and my feelings and made the same selfish mistakes he did in the beginning of our marriage. There had been no growth on his part and it made me feel even lonelier and unloved. I was doing all of the emotional work and receiving nothing in return. It's when women feel lonely, unappreciated and neglected that they're most prone to cheat. After confessing how lonely I felt, he admitted to not being there and for some time, worked to make things better. But nothing ever lasted for long. He returned to his old habits. And I returned to mine...doing whatever I could to get him to love me.

I was truly dumbfounded. I believed if I changed for the better, he would change too. Albeit, I wasn't perfect and he knew it. But I was transparent and apologetic. I wanted him to feel loved even when I was wrong. It changed nothing. After months of counseling, my therapist suggested that nothing would ever change and I should give up. This infuriated me because I still believed in forever. She explained there was nothing I could do or say to get someone to change. She threw in the word narcissism and because I was unfamiliar with the term, I did my research. And it all made sense. Still, I refused to give up. I read narcissists don't change and aren't receptive to counseling, but I believed in God. He could reach my husband and allow miracles to happen in his life as well. During this marriage, I forgave my abusers. I learned to love a man who didn't love me. And I became a better parent, wife, sister, and friend.

    All my life, I had heard the cliche "stress kills" but I had always dismissed it as an exaggeration. But a brain aneurysm I suffered was brought on by stress. My girlfriend was murdered and my husband had been giving me the silent treatment for over a month. He had become increasingly turbulent since I refused to give in to his martyrdom; I simply didn't have it in me. Plus, it forced me to see that not only did he not love me, he didn't care enough about me to comfort me during my grief. Instead, he began to intimidate me physically and I was expecting him to hit me or hit me with something any day. He had done it before; we weren't yet married when it happened but I had explained to him how it made me feel and that I would leave if he ever did it again. He didn't so I believed throughout our 12 year marriage, his boiling rage had been squelched. But when he forcefully pushed the door just inches away from my face and laughed at my fear, I knew it was time for me to go. I rented an apartment and told him I wouldn't return until he sought anger management counseling. I understood domestic violence to be a progression. Most men don't start off hitting their spouse; they work their way up to it. And his anger had started to be expressed physically.

In the ER, when the doctors learned of my recent stress, they suggested I relax and closed the door so my husband and I could have some time alone. Once the doors closed, my husband grabbed my hand and I heard him cry softly. But again, it changed nothing. Once I was discharged, my husband never reached out to me. We were together at our son's sporting events, but he wouldn't talk to me nor make eye contact. It's like he was taking his anger out on me as if I did something wrong. I had explained to him why I left and reassured him often that I would return home after he completed anger management. He claimed to understand but after a few months into the separation, he *told* our son to relay a message to me: he found a woman he wanted to marry and he wanted a divorce.

    I was devastated and felt misled by God. It was my understanding that because divorce is a sin, God would turn things around and I would be rewarded for my obedience. Why would God allow divorce to take place? Why would he allow me to marry him in the first place? And why when I learned to love did he leave? It would not have hurt so badly if we divorced during the period I resented him. My heart ached because after doing (almost) everything right, he chose to walk away. After contemplation, research, and prayer, I realized that God has given us the freedom to choose but His ultimate will is for us to walk in integrity, follow His principles, use wisdom, and seek Him in all things. Although I didn't do everything right during my marriage, it was the catalyst to recognizing and submitting to His ultimate will. And yes, God does hate divorce, but everyday, He forgives us for our sins. While my marriage wasn't ordained, it brought me, His prodigal daughter, home so I will always be eternally grateful for the union...and its ending. I could have easily died from the aneurysm or remained married and died from the effects of stress.

If you've found yourself separated or divorced, please look for the lesson and know that in every mistake and misguided decision we make, He forgives and loves us through it.

Afterword

It's spring 2017 and I'm sitting on Amanda's bed in California shocked by the stories she's relaying to me. We had been friends since 2005 and over the years, we both felt that something was just not right with our husbands. Mine had left in 2014 and while I was fully healed, Amanda was just beginning her healing journey. She did appear happier, relaxed and more peaceful than I ever saw her but she admitted to needing to be deprogrammed from all of the abuse she suffered. Not quite sure how she was going to manage everything financially, I assured her, "hun, this was a blessing in disguise. You don't know how many times I wished you were divorced with me. You deserve so much better than him."

And that's when it hit me. Excited, I shared with her the idea for this book. I was going to give it the title, "Blessing In Disguise: How Divorce Became My

Deliverance." She immediately agreed to participate and after talking to a few more friends, my random idea was turning into a reality. I advertised on social media and by the grace of God, found some incredible women from across America with unbelievable stories. We were all excited, not about sharing our business, but for the chance to use our experiences to help others. It may be hard to believe if you're currently in an unhealthy marriage or if you never experienced physical or emotional abuse, but once you're free, there's a feeling of serenity and strength you never knew existed. That's probably because our spouses did everything they could to keep us from recognizing our power and using our voices to speak up.

As I read each story, I began to notice a trend among us all. We were all victims of similar types of misbehavior. In the chart below, the authors of the various chapters took time to list the behaviors we all endured during our marriage. The numbers one through nine are indicative of each chapter and the respective author.

Behavior	1	2	3	4	5	6	7	8	9
Emotional Abuse	X	X	X	X	X	X	X	X	X
Financial Abuse		X	X			X	X		X
Infidelity		X		X	X		X	X	
Physical Abuse		X		X		X	X		
Quick Marriage	X					X	X	X	X
Verbal Abuse	X	X	X	X		X	X		X

As the chart shows, the common thread among us all was being victims of emotional abuse, a form of abuse in which a partner uses verbal assault, fear, or humiliation to undermine the other person's self-esteem and self-worth. As you read, it can be just as damaging as physical abuse. It poisoned our marriages and negatively altered our self-perception, self-worth, and self-confidence. We spent most of our married years believing we were worthless and *un*deserving of love and respect. But we weren't. We were simply *un*appreciated and *un*loved.

If you are separated or recently divorced, I pray these stories gave you the strength to persevere. Yes, it may be an emotional or financial struggle, but things will get better. Do the work necessary to heal. Mourn the death of your marriage. Nurture your children as they navigate weekend visits, new schools and the disappointment of no longer having both parents in the home. Whether or not there was abuse, the marriage ended for a reason. And I guarantee you, in time, you'll realize it was a blessing in disguise.

Elona Washington, MSM

Freedom aka After the Divorce

Freedom from hurt and pain

Free to be me

Freedom from abuse

After the divorce...

Freedom from being lied to

Free to love

Freedom from being cheated on

After the divorce...

Freedom from a strong fist

Free to love God

Freedom from lazy arms and legs

After the divorce...

Freedom from hurtful words

Free to love others

Freedom from emotional roller coasters

After the divorce...

Freedom from fighting and struggling

Free to love ME

Freedom to be free, move free, live free

Free to be me

After the divorce...

C. Michelle Atkins

Freedom aka After The Divorce is from the book entitled, *Tales from My Life, not the Crypt*, by C. Michelle Atkins, copyright 2014.

Get Support

Andrea M. Stuckey, Live Life Luvd Coaching
http://www.livelifeluvd.com

Day One Emotional Abuse Hotline
https://www.dayoneservices.org

The National Domestic Violence Hotline
http://www.thehotline.org/

Rape Abuse Incest National Network (RAINN)
https://www.rainn.org/

National Suicide Prevention Hotline
https://suicidepreventionlifeline.org/

About The Authors

Lisa McGovern is a pen name; she asked to remain anonymous.

Dannielle Brown is a Master's in Counseling Psychology candidate.

Amanda Garcia is a pen name; she asked to remain anonymous.

C. Michelle Atkins is an author and poet and all of her works are available on her Amazon page.

Lori Obayomi is an entrepreneur and author.

Nisha is an urban fiction author whose works can be found on her Amazon page.

Stephanie Thomas is a thought curator, writer and author. She can be reached at www.authorstephaniethomas.com.

Tracee Upton is a pen name; she asked to remain anonymous.

Elona Washington is an author and the publisher of this anthology. Visit www.elonawashington.com for more information.

www.ingramcontent.com/pod-product-compliance
Lightning Source LLC
Chambersburg PA
CBHW060537100426
42743CB00009B/1559